Collins

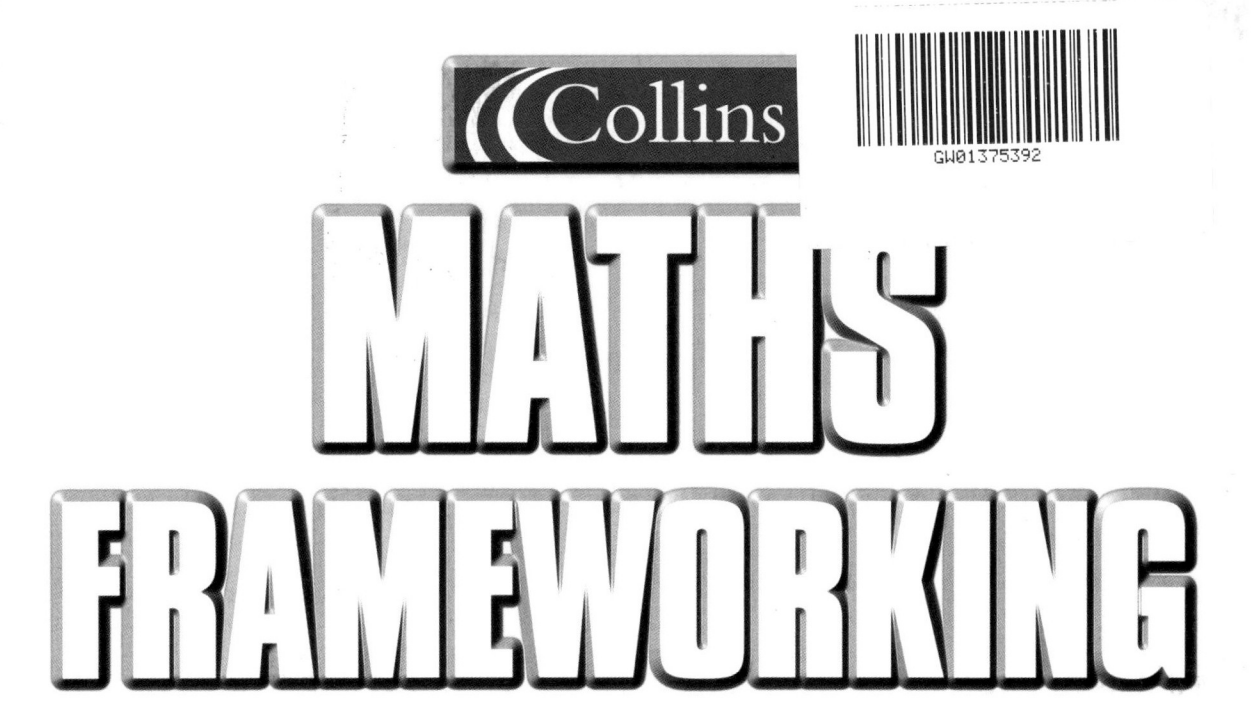

MATHS FRAMEWORKING

Complete success for Mathematics at KS3

YEAR 8   PRACTICE BOOK 1

ANDREW EDMONDSON

Contents

Chapter 1	**Number and Algebra 1**	5
Chapter 2	**Shape, Space and Measures 1**	10
Chapter 3	**Handling Data 1**	15
Chapter 4	**Number 2**	18
Chapter 5	**Algebra 2**	22
Chapter 6	**Shape, Space and Measures 2**	25
Chapter 7	**Algebra 3**	31
Chapter 8	**Number 3**	35
Chapter 9	**Shape, Space and Measures 3**	40
Chapter 10	**Algebra 4**	44
Chapter 11	**Handling Data 2**	48
Chapter 12	**Number 4**	52
Chapter 13	**Algebra 5**	55
Chapter 14	**Solving Problems**	60
Chapter 15	**Shape, Space and Measures 4**	63
Chapter 16	**Handling Data 3**	69

CHAPTER 1: Number and Algebra 1

Practice

1A Negative numbers

1 Work out the answer to each of these.
- **a** $-5 + 8$
- **b** $2 - 7$
- **c** $-4 - 9$
- **d** $2 - 6 - 3$
- **e** $-5 + 6 - 4$
- **f** $-3 + 8 - 2$

2 Work out the answer to each of these.
- **a** $5 - +7$
- **b** $-7 + -3$
- **c** $4 - -6$
- **d** $-3 - +4$
- **e** $-5 - -4$
- **f** $- +7 - 4 + 6$
- **g** $2 - -5 - -8$
- **h** $-4 + -6 - + 3$

3 Find the missing numbers to make these true.
- **a** $-5 + \square = -3$
- **b** $\square - 3 = -7$
- **c** $\square - -3 = 0$
- **d** $-2 - \square = 6$

4 Calculate these.
- **a** $5 - 9$
- **b** $2 - 6 + 3$
- **c** $-2 + -5$
- **d** $9 - -7$
- **e** $-3 - +5 - 4$

5

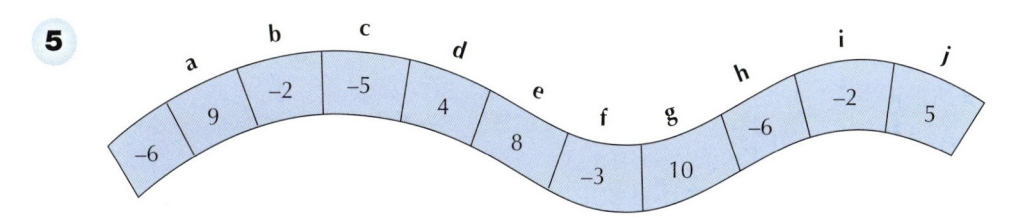

Numbers around the curve: a = −6, b = 9, c = −2, d = −5, e = 4, f = 8, g = −3, h = 10, i = −6, j = −2, k = 5

- **i** Add each number to the number on its left. Write down your answers. For example, **a** $-6 + 9 = ?$
- **ii** Subtract each number from the number on its left. Write down your answers. For example, **a** $-6 - 9 = ?$

6 Calculate these.
- **a** 5×-3
- **b** -8×-5
- **c** -3×10
- **d** -2×-2
- **e** 14×-3
- **f** $-4 \times -2 \times 5$
- **g** $2 \times -3 \times -1$
- **h** $-10 \times 6 \times -10$

7 Calculate these.
- **a** $16 \div -2$
- **b** $-6 \div -6$
- **c** $-9 \div 3$
- **d** $12 \div -3$
- **e** $-100 \div 10$
- **f** $20 \div -2 \div -5$
- **g** $-36 \div -3 \div -4$
- **h** $40 \div -5 \div -2$

8 Copy and complete these chains of calculations.

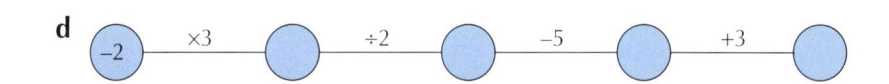

a −2 →+3→ ○ →−5→ ○ →−2→ ○ →+1→ ○

b −1 →×4→ ○ →×−2→ ○ →−3→ ○ →+5→ ○

c 6 →×−2→ ○ →+7→ ○ →−3→ ○ →×−3→ ○

d −2 →×3→ ○ →÷2→ ○ →−5→ ○ →+3→ ○

1B HCF and LCM

1 a Write the first 10 multiples of these numbers.
   i 3   **ii** 6
   iii 10   **iv** 12

  b Use your answers to **a** to find the LCM of these pairs of numbers.
   i 3 and 8   **ii** 6 and 12
   iii 6 and 10   **iv** 10 and 12

2 a Write out all the factors of these numbers.
   i 12   **ii** 18
   iii 20 **iv** 30

  b Use your answers to **a** to find the HCF of these pairs of numbers.
   i 12 and 18   **ii** 12 and 20
   iii 20 and 30 **iv** 18 and 20

3 Find the LCM of these pairs of numbers
   Hint: Write out the first few multiples of each number.

   a 4 and 8   **b** 6 and 10
   c 7 and 8   **d** 9 and 12

4 Find the HCF of these pairs of numbers.
   Hint: Write the factors of each number.

   a 14 and 35   **b** 8 and 20
   c 12 and 30   **d** 15 and 24

1C Powers and roots

1 Write down the values of the following. Do not use a calculator.

   a $\sqrt{64}$ **b** $\sqrt{1}$ **c** $\sqrt{121}$
   d $\sqrt{81}$ **e** $\sqrt{0}$

2 Calculate these. Do not use a calculator.

  a $\sqrt{9} \times \sqrt{16}$ **b** $\sqrt{81} \times \sqrt{4}$
  c $\sqrt{100} \div \sqrt{25}$ **d** $\sqrt{9} \times \sqrt{16} \div \sqrt{36}$

3 With the aid of a calculator, write down the value of these square roots.

  a $\sqrt{196}$ **b** $\sqrt{784}$ **c** $\sqrt{8281}$
  d $\sqrt{344\,569}$ **e** $\sqrt{33\,640\,000}$

4 Make an estimate of these square roots, then use the calculator to see how were right.

  a $\sqrt{169}$ **b** $\sqrt{484}$ **c** $\sqrt{900}$
  d $\sqrt{3600}$ **e** $\sqrt{2209}$

5 Use your calculator to work out these square roots. Round your answers to the nearest whole number.

  a $\sqrt{200}$ **b** $\sqrt{13}$
  c $\sqrt{732}$ **d** $\sqrt{8000}$

6 Sometimes, the differences between two square numbers is another square number. For example, $10^2 - 8^2 = 100 - 64 = 36$, which is a square number. Use the numbers in the cloud to find more of these.
Write each answer like this: $10^2 - 8^2 = 6^2$.

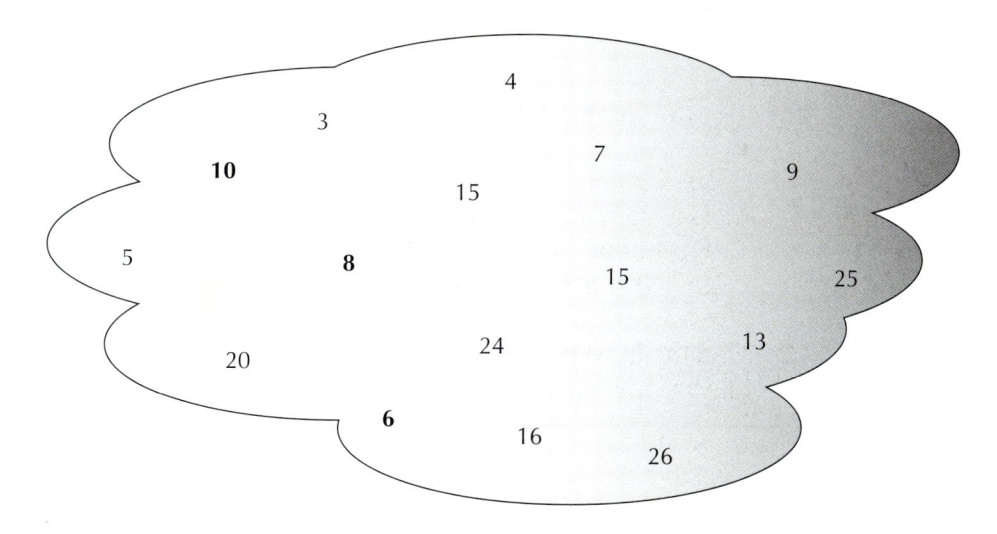

Cloud contains: 3, 4, 5, 6, 7, 8, 9, 10, 13, 15, 15, 16, 20, 24, 25, 26

7 a Copy and continue this pattern to make eight rows. Work out all of the answers.

  1   =
  1 + 3   =
  1 + 3 + 5   =
  1 + 3 + 5 + …   =

  b What can you say about the answers?
  c Can you find a rule that gives the answer? Check that your rule works.

Practice
1D Prime factors

1 These are the products of prime factors of some numbers.
What are the numbers?

   a $2 \times 5 \times 5$ **b** $2 \times 2 \times 2 \times 3$ **c** $2 \times 3 \times 7 \times 7$

2 Use a prime factor tree to write each of these numbers as a product of its prime factors.

   a   6   **b**   18   **c**   32
   d   70   **e**   36

3 Use a prime factor tree to write each of these numbers as a product of its prime factors. Start your diagram with the numbers in brackets.

   a   100 (4 × 25)   **b**   128 (8 × 16)   **c**   180 (10 × 18)
   d   135 (9 × 15)   **e**   132 (6 × 22)   **f**   210 (10 × 21)

Practice
1E Sequences 1

1 Follow the instructions to generate sequences.

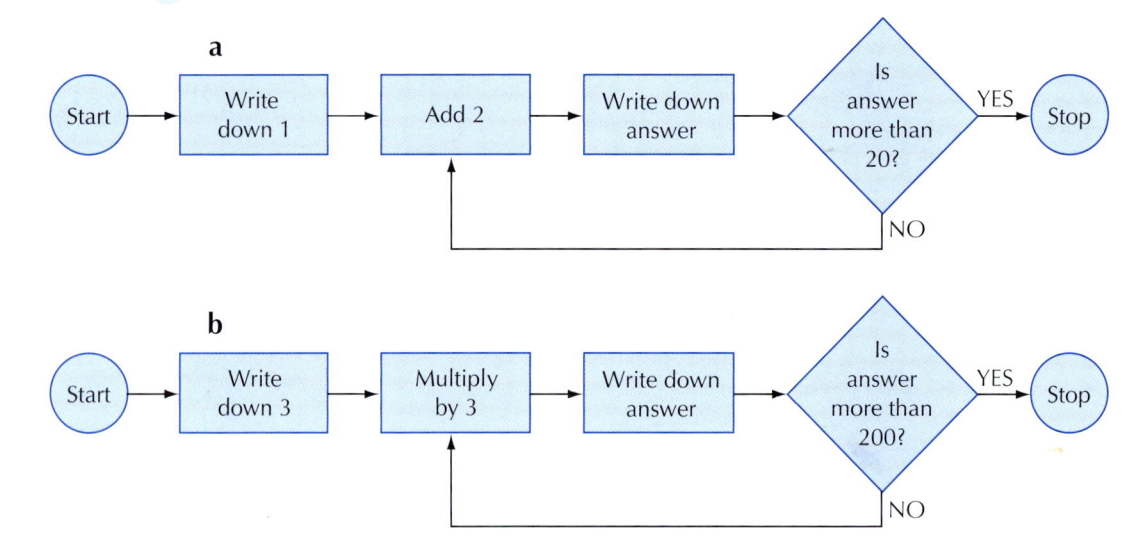

a Start → Write down 1 → Add 2 → Write down answer → Is answer more than 20? — YES → Stop; NO → back to Add 2

b Start → Write down 3 → Multiply by 3 → Write down answer → Is answer more than 200? — YES → Stop; NO → back to Multiply by 3

2 Draw a flow diagram to generate the sequence that starts with 10 and uses the term-to-term rule 'add 5'.

3 a Describe how these sequences are generated.
    i   5, 8, 11, 14, 17 …
    ii   30, 28, 26, 24 …
    iii   2, 10, 50, 250 …
b Find the next two numbers in each sequence.

4 Given the start and term-to-term rule, write down the first five terms of each of these sequences.

    a Start 8, rule: add 4   **b** Start 50, rule: subtract 5
    c Start 3, rule: multiply by 4   **d** Start 64, rule: divide by 2

5 These patterns of dots generate sequences of numbers.

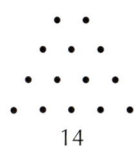

    a   4   7   10   13

    b   2   5   9   14

    i For each sequence, draw the next two patterns of dots.
    ii Write down the next four numbers in each sequence.

1F Sequences 2

1 You are given the first term and the term-to-term rule. Write down the first five terms of each sequence.

    a First term 2, term-to-term-rule: multiply by 5
    b First term 3, term-to-term-rule: multiply by 2 then add 4
    c First term 5, term-to-term-rule: subtract 1, then multiply by 2

2 Copy and complete the table for each sequence.

    a Rule: multiply term position number by 3.

Term position number, n	1	2	3	4	5
Term		6			

    b Rule: multiply term position number by 4 then subtract 1.

Term position number, n	1	2	3	4	5
Term		7			

3 The nth term of each sequence is given below.

    a $3n - 1$ **b** $2n + 5$ **c** $5n - 3$ **d** $10n + 10$

Copy and complete this table for each sequence.

Term position number, n	1	2	3	4	5
Term					

Practice

1G Solving problems

1 Paving slabs 1 metre square are used for borders around L-shaped ponds.

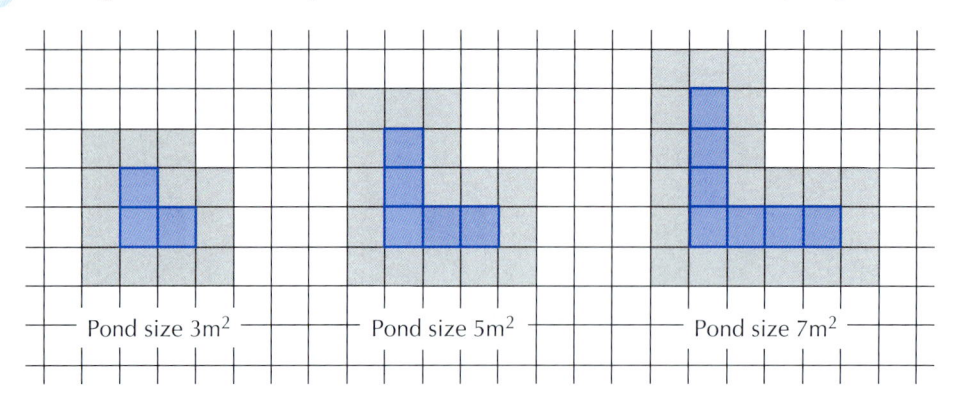

Pond size 3m²   Pond size 5m²   Pond size 7m²

   a How many slabs would fit around a pond of size 9 square metres?
   b Write a rule to show the number of slabs needed to make a border around L-shaped ponds.

2 Write a rule to show the number of matches needed to make these shapes.

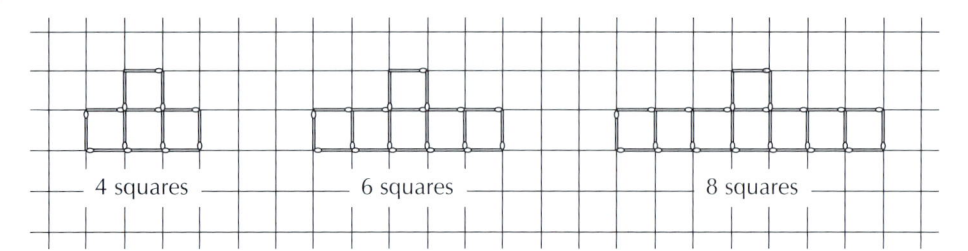

4 squares   6 squares   8 squares

CHAPTER 2
Shape, Space and Measures 1

Practice

2A Parallel and perpendicular lines

1   **i**   Which of these sets of lines are parallel?

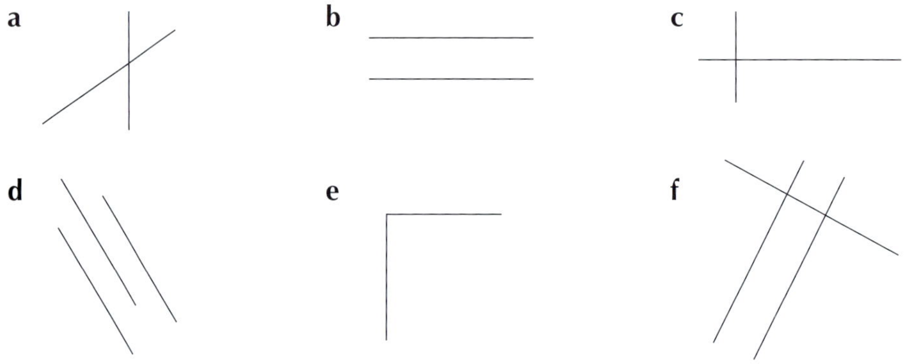

    a   **b**   **c**

    d   **e**   **f**

   ii   Which of the sets of lines are perpendicular?

2 a Copy each of these lines on to square dotted paper.
On each diagram, draw two more lines that are parallel to the first line.

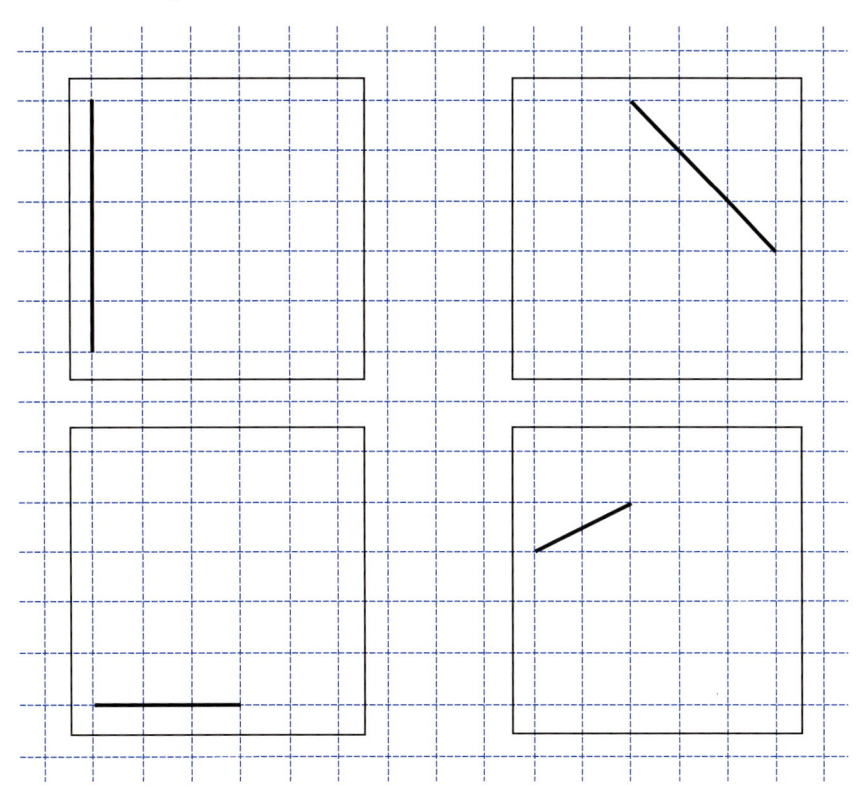

b Copy each of the lines again on to square dotted paper.
On each diagram, draw two more lines that are perpendicular to the first line.

3 Look at this diagram.

a Which lines are parallel to the line AB?
b Which lines are perpendicular to the line AB?

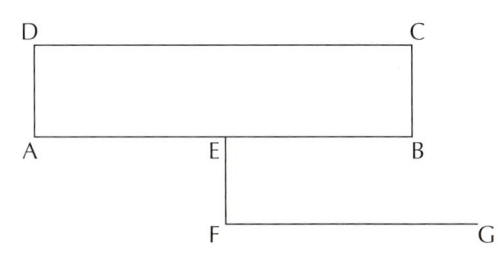

Practice

2B Measuring and drawing angles

1 Describe each of these angles as acute, right-angled, obtuse or reflex.

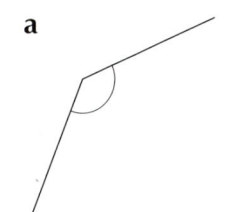

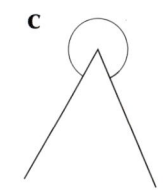

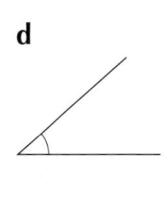

a   b   c   d

2 Measure the size of each of these angles, giving your answers correct to the nearest degree.

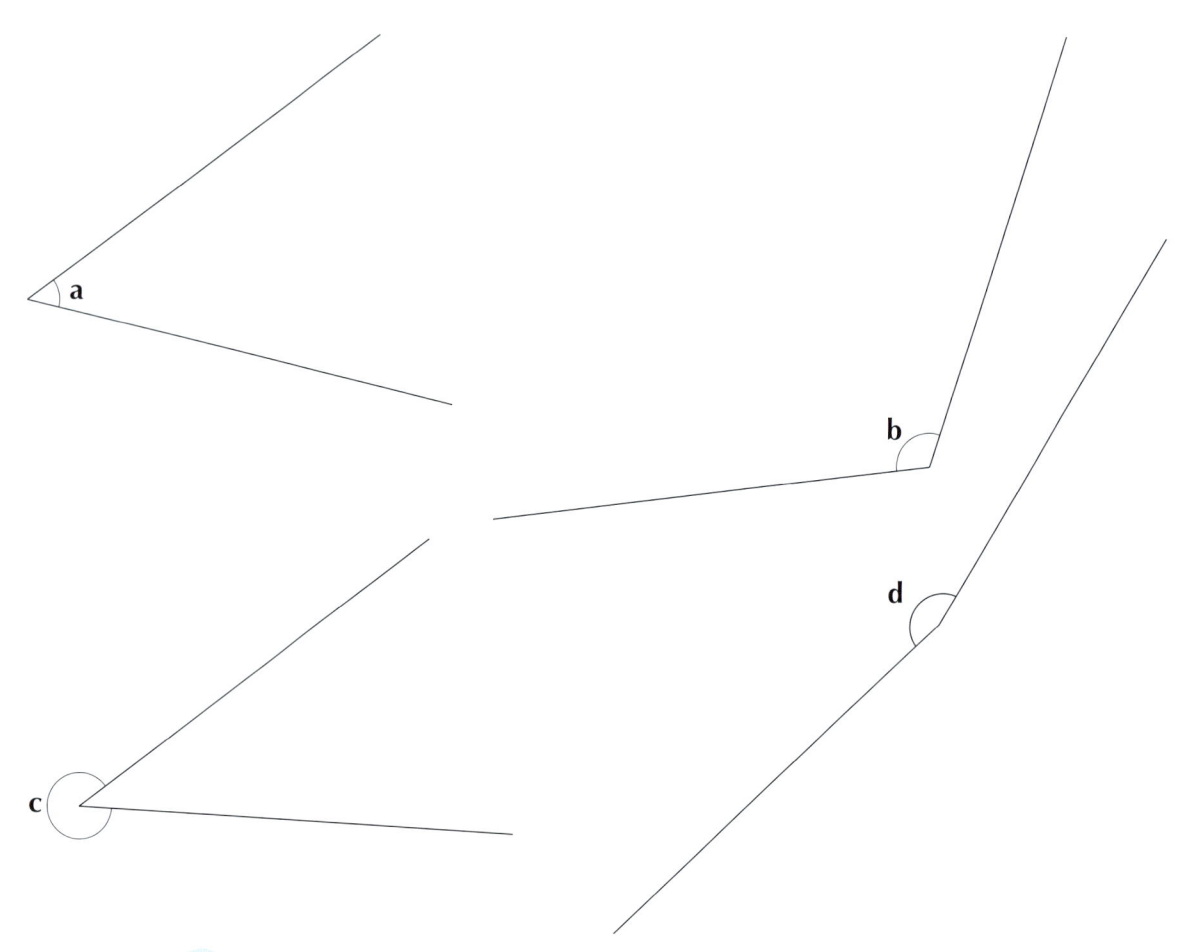

3 Draw and label these angles.

    a 70°   **b** 35°   **c** 135°
    d 200°   **e** 340°

4 Measure the four angles in quadrilateral ABCD.

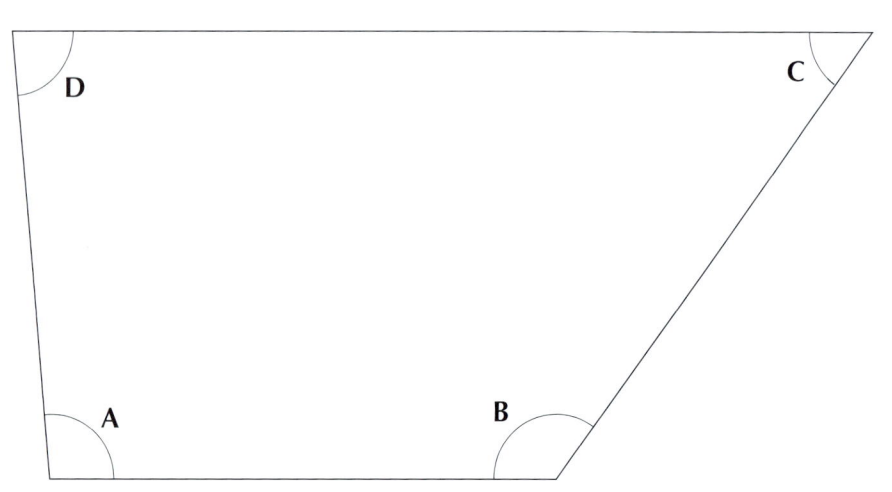

Practice

2C Calculating angles

Calculate the size of each unknown angle.

1 a, b, 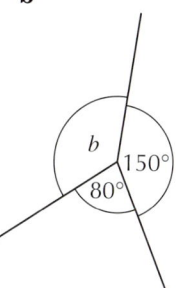 c

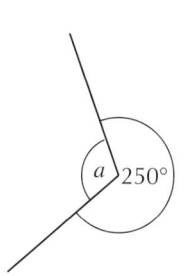

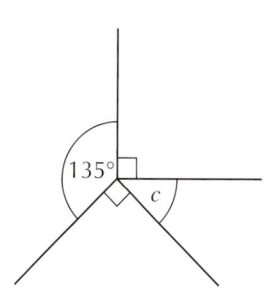

(a: 250° reflex; b: 150° and 80° given; c: 135° and right angle given)

2 a, 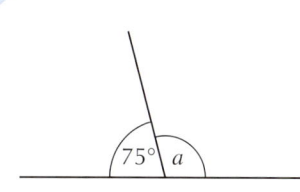 b, 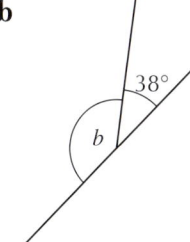 c

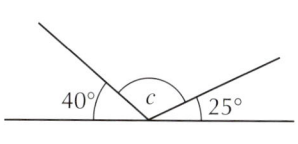

(a: 75°; b: 38°; c: 40° and 25°)

3 a, 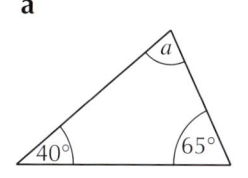 b, 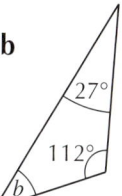 c

(a: 40°, 65°; b: 27°, 112°; c: right angle, 52°)

4 a, 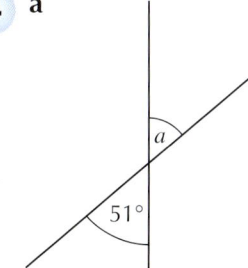 b, 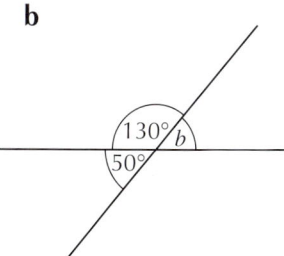 c

(a: 51°; b: 130°, 50°; c: 86°, 36°, 58°)

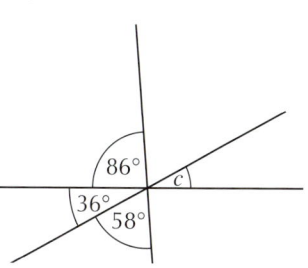

Practice

2D The geometric properties of quadrilaterals

1 Copy this table, and in each column, write the names of all possible quadrilaterals that could fit the description.

2 pairs of equal angles	Rotational symmetry of order 4	Exactly 1 line of symmetry	Exactly 2 right angles	Exactly 4 equal sides
	Square			

Warning: A quadrilateral could be in more than one column!

13

2 a Some quadrilaterals have two pairs of equal angles. Which are they?
b Some quadrilaterals have two pairs of equal sides. Which are they?

3 a A quadrilateral has exactly two equal angles.
What type of quadrilateral could it be?
b A quadrilateral has three equal angles.
What type of quadrilateral could it be?

4 Some quadrilaterals have diagonals that intersect at right angles.
Find as many as you can. Illustrate your answers with drawings.

Practice — 2E Constructions

1 Construct these triangles. **Remember:** Label the vertices and angles.

a Triangle ABC with BC = 6 cm, AC = 5 cm, ∠C = 40°.

b Triangle DEF with DE = 5 cm, EF = 8 cm, ∠E = 120°.

c Triangle GHI with GH = 5.2 cm, HI = 4.8 cm, ∠H = 90°.

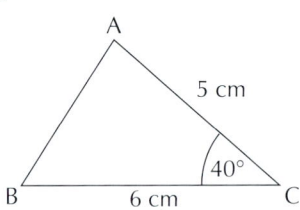

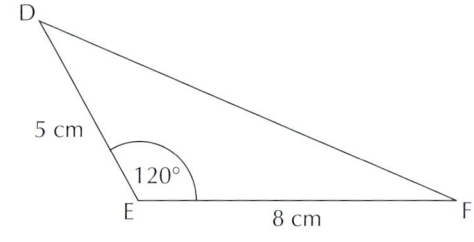

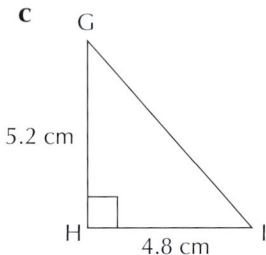

2 Construct these triangles. **Remember:** Label the vertices and angles.

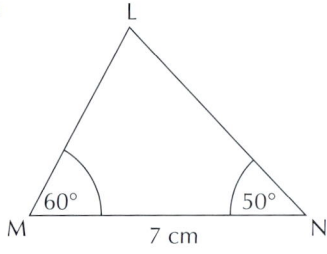

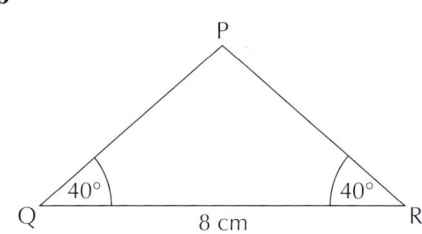

a Triangle LMN with MN = 7 cm, ∠M = 60°, ∠N = 50°.

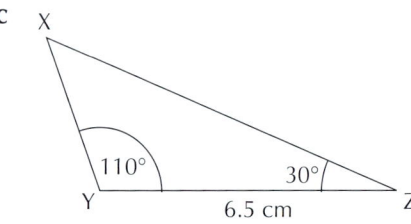

b Triangle PQR with QR = 8 cm, ∠Q = 40°, ∠R = 40°.

c Triangle XYZ with YZ = 6.5 cm, ∠Y = 110°, ∠Z = 30°.

3 a Construct the triangle ABC, with AB = 6 cm, BC = 11.5 cm and ∠B = 35°.
b Measure side AC, giving your answer correct to the nearest millimetre.

CHAPTER 3 Handling Data 1

Practice

3A Probability

1 Copy this scale.

|—————|—————|—————|—————|
Impossible   Unlikely   Evens   Likely   Certain

Label your scale with each of these events.
a Choosing an ace from a pack of 52 cards – there are 4 aces in a pack.
b You will experience it raining some time in the future.
c You are travelling down an unknown road. The next bend is left.
d A person can walk on water unaided.
e A wine glass breaks when you drop it onto the floor.

2 Write down an event that is

a unlikely   b certain   c likely   d impossible

3 A child is asked to choose a lucky number from one of these:

1   2   3   4   5   6   7   8   9

Which of these is more likely to be chosen?
a An odd number or number less than 5
b A prime number or even number
c A multiple of 3 or multiple of 4
d A triangle number or cube number

4 Imagine these quadrilaterals are cut from plastic and placed in a bag.

rectangle   parallelogram   square   rhombus   kite   trapezium

You choose one at random.
Copy and complete these sentences by filling in the missing probability words: impossible, unlikely, evens, likely, certain.

a Picking a shape with a right angle is ___.
b Picking a shape with at least two equal sides is ___.
c Picking a shape with four angles is ___.
d Picking a shape with four equal angles is ___.
e Picking a shape with no equal sides is ___.
f Picking a shape with only three sides is ___.

3B Probability scales

1 100 rings are placed in a box. 20 are gold, 25 are silver, 16 are plastic and the rest are copper. A ring is chosen at random.
What is the probability of choosing this kind of ring?

    a gold   **b** silver   **c** plastic   **d** copper
    e not gold   **f** not silver   **g** not plastic   **h** not copper

2 This diagram shows 12 dominoes.

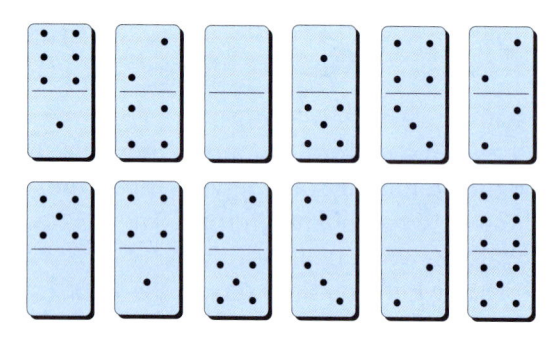

A domino is chosen at random. Calculate these probabilities.

    a It has a 5   **b** It is a double
    c It has a total of 7   **d** It is not a double
    e It does not have a 5   **f** It does not have a blank
    g It does not have a 3

3 The probability that a large egg box contains a cracked egg is 0.12.
What is the probability that a large egg box does *not* contain a cracked egg?

4 Copy and complete this table.

Event	Probability of event occurring (p)	Probability of event not occurring ($1 - p$)
A	$\frac{2}{5}$	$1 - \frac{2}{5} =$
B	0.75	
C	$\frac{1}{4}$	
D	0.1	
E	$\frac{19}{20}$	
F	0.8	
G	$\frac{5}{8}$	

5 A weather forecaster estimates the probability of rain to be 0.35, black ice $\frac{4}{5}$, and a 1 in 10 chance of snow. What is the probability of

    a no snow?   **b** no black ice?   **c** no rain?

Practice
3C Experimental probability

1 The numbers of days it rained over different periods are recorded in this table.

Recording period	Number of days of rain	Experimental probability
30	12	12 ÷ 30 = 0.4
60	33	
100	42	
200	90	
500	235	

   a Copy and complete the table.
   b What is the best estimate of the probability of it raining? Explain your answer.
   c Estimate the probability of it not raining.
   d Is there a greater chance of it raining or not raining?

2 If you drop a matchbox, it can land in one of three positions.

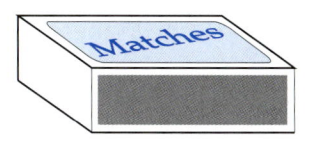

END   EDGE   SIDE

   a Drop a matchbox 10 times. Copy this tally chart and record your results.

How matchbox landed	Tally	Frequency	Experimental probability
End			
Edge			
Side			

   b Calculate the experimental probabilities.
   c Repeat the experiment. This time drop the matchbox 20 times.
   d Repeat the experiment with 50 trials.
   e Which is the best estimate of the probability of the matchbox landing
      i on end?
      ii on edge?
      iii on a side?
   f Compare your estimated probabilities with your classmates.

CHAPTER 4 Number 2

Practice
4A Fractions and decimals

1 Cancel these fractions to their simplest form.

a $\frac{5}{20}$ b $\frac{10}{12}$ c $\frac{21}{35}$

d $\frac{16}{20}$ e $\frac{12}{18}$ f $\frac{30}{25}$

2 Write these decimals as fractions with a denominator of 10 or 100. Then cancel to their simplest form.

a 0.7   b 0.15   c 0.2   d 0.65
e 0.8   f 0.24   g 0.06   h 0.64
i 0.02   j 0.55

3 Convert these fractions to decimals.

a $\frac{7}{10}$ b $\frac{13}{100}$ c $\frac{3}{10}$ d $\frac{1}{4}$

e $\frac{97}{100}$ f $\frac{1}{2}$ g $\frac{1}{10}$ h $\frac{9}{100}$

i $\frac{17}{50}$ j $\frac{3}{100}$

4 Convert these fractions to decimals. Change each denominator to 100 first.

a $\frac{7}{50}$ b $\frac{9}{20}$ c $\frac{8}{25}$

d $\frac{27}{50}$ e $\frac{13}{20}$

Practice
4B Adding and subtracting fractions

For Questions 1–3, if necessary, cancel your answers and write the answers as mixed numbers.

1 a $\frac{3}{7} + \frac{2}{7}$ b $\frac{5}{9} + \frac{1}{9}$ c $\frac{1}{12} + \frac{5}{12}$

d $\frac{5}{8} + \frac{1}{8}$ e $\frac{7}{8} + \frac{7}{8}$ f $\frac{3}{10} + \frac{9}{10} + \frac{7}{10}$

2 a $\frac{4}{5} - \frac{1}{5}$ b $\frac{8}{9} - \frac{5}{9}$ c $\frac{7}{8} - \frac{3}{8}$

d $\frac{9}{10} - \frac{3}{10}$ e $\frac{11}{12} - \frac{3}{12}$

3 a $\frac{4}{7} + \frac{4}{7}$ b $\frac{7}{9} - \frac{1}{9}$ c $\frac{3}{8} + \frac{7}{8}$

d $\frac{11}{6} - \frac{7}{6}$ e $\frac{1}{3} + \frac{2}{3} + \frac{2}{3}$ f $\frac{13}{15} - \frac{8}{15}$

g $\frac{5}{6} + \frac{5}{6} - \frac{1}{6}$

4 Calculate these.

a $\frac{4}{9}$ of 36 kg b $\frac{5}{6}$ of 30 ml c $\frac{2}{7}$ of 28 cm

5 Work out these. Cancel your answers and write the answers as mixed numbers if necessary.

a $2 \times \frac{3}{8}$ b $4 \times \frac{3}{7}$ c $9 \times \frac{5}{6}$

d $7 \times \frac{2}{5}$ e $6 \times \frac{8}{9}$

Practice — 4C Fractions and percentages

Do not use a calculator. Show your working.

1 Write these fractions as percentages.
Convert each denominator to 100 first, if necessary.

a $\frac{49}{100}$ b $\frac{7}{100}$ c $\frac{21}{50}$ d $\frac{13}{25}$ e $\frac{11}{20}$

2 What is

a 7 as a percentage of 10? b 19 as a percentage of 25?
c 13 as a percentage of 20? d 33 as a percentage of 50?
e 3 as a percentage of 5? f 1 as a percentage of 20?

3 Milton drinks 27 cl of a 50-cl bottle of orange.

a What percentage did he drink?
b What percentage remains?

4 A company employs 25 workers. At the last general election, 13 voted Labour, 10 voted Liberal Democrat and the remainder voted Conservative. Calculate the percentage vote for each party.

5 Stuart took a maths test lasting 20 minutes.
He spent 8 minutes on the Algebra section, 7 minutes on the Number section and the remaining time on the Shape and Space section.
What percentage of the time did he spend on each section?

6 16 out of 25 pupils in class 8A passed their maths test. 13 out of 20 pupils in class 8B passed the same maths test. Which class had the better results?
Hint: Calculate the percentage for each class.

4D Percentage increase and decrease

Do not use a calculator. Show your working.

1 Calculate these.
- **a** 20% of £80
- **b** 5% of 20 kg
- **c** 15% of 140 cm
- **d** 90% of 400 litres

2 Mrs Walker left £45 000 in her will. The money was divided between her three children as follows.

Derek 60%
Maria 25%
Jason 15%

How much did each child receive?

3 Three people each withdrew a certain percentage of their bank balance from their bank account:

John withdrew 30% of £300
Hans withdrew 75% of £640
Will withdrew 15% of £280

- **a** How much did each person withdraw?
- **b** Which person has the largest remaining bank balance?

4
- **a** Increase $40 by 20%
- **b** Decrease 200 kg by 5%
- **c** Decrease 70p by 60%
- **d** Increase 2000 m by 25%
- **e** Increase 140 ml by 15%
- **f** Decrease £250 by 20%

5 Before a typing course, Leon could type 60 words per minute. The typing course increased his speed by 15%. What was his speed after the course?

6 'Zipping' a computer file reduces its size by a certain percentage. Find the sizes of these files after zipping.
- **a** 500kB file reduced by 20%
- **b** 740kB file reduced by 5%
- **c** 840kB file reduced by 25%
- **d** 1900kB file reduced by 90%

7 Marvin's average score on the computer game Space Attack was 150.
- **a** After buying a new gamepad, his average score increased by 20%. What was his new average score?
- **b** Marvin went on holiday. When he returned, his average score had decreased by 15%. What was his new average score?

Practice

4E Real-life problems

1 Dan bought a calculator from a shop for £23. The shopkeeper paid £20 for the calculator. What percentage profit did the shopkeeper make?

2 Maria bought a skateboard for £25. She sold it two months later for £18. What was her percentage loss?

3 An odd job man kept a record of his income and costs for each job. Copy and complete this table.

Job	Costs (£)	Income (£)	Profit (£)	Percentage profit (%)
4 Down Close	100	135		
High Birches	50	91		
27 Bowden Rd	25	42		
Church hall	20	34		

4 Three dealers offer the following repayment options for a car with a marked price of £12 000. Which works out the cheapest overall?

Trustworthy Cars   20% deposit followed by 12 monthly payments of £900
Bargain Autos   15% deposit followed by 8 monthly payments of £1400
Future Car Sales   25% deposit followed by 6 monthly payments of £1650

5 Amanda deposited £30 000 in her bank. The bank pays interest of 10% per annum.

   a Show that Amanda had £33 000 in her bank account after one year.
   b Amanda kept all of the money in her bank for another 3 years. Copy and complete this table.

Year	Amount at beginning of year (£)	Interest earned at 10% per annum	Amount at end of year (£)
1	30 000	10% of 30 000 =	33 000
2	33 000		
3			
4			

6 Hamid weighed 50 kg before he went on a diet. After the diet, he weighed 46 kg. What was his percentage loss in weight?

CHAPTER 5 Algebra 2

Practice
5A Algebraic shorthand

1 Write each of these expressions using algebraic shorthand.
- **a** $x \div 5$
- **b** $3 \times b$
- **c** $m \div n$
- **d** $p \times 3$
- **e** $y \div 4$

2 Copy and complete these.
- **a** $8 + 3 = 3 + \square$
- **b** $\square \times 2 = 2 \times 6$
- **c** $a + b = b + \square$
- **d** $4 \times s = s \times \square$
- **e** $\square \times h = ht$
- **f** $8r = r \times \square$
- **g** $pq = \square \times q$

3 Simplify these.
- **a** $4 \times 2 \times s$
- **b** $5 \times 3d$
- **c** $t \times 2 \times 3$
- **d** $5m \times 5$
- **e** $a \times 2 \times 2$

4 Solve each of these equations.
- **a** $x + 7 = 10$
- **b** $x - 3 = 6$
- **c** $x + 1 = 15$
- **d** $x - 8 = 8$
- **e** $x - 10 = 20$
- **f** $x + 13 = 40$

5 Find the expressions that are equal. Write them as an equation, e.g. $4 + s = s + 4$.
- **a** $5y, y + 5, y \times 5$
- **b** $5 + p, 5p, p - 5, p + 5$
- **c** $a - b, ab, a + b, a \times b$
- **d** $\frac{3}{h}, h \div 3h, \frac{h}{3}$

Practice
5B Like terms

1 Simplify these expressions.
- **a** $f + f$
- **b** $i + i + i + i$
- **c** $H + H + H$
- **d** $m + m + m + m + m + m$
- **e** $u + u + u + u + u + u + u + u + u + u + u + u$

2 Write out these in full, e.g. $3t = t + t + t$.
- **a** $4d$
- **b** $6a$
- **c** $8G$

3 Simplify these expressions.
- **a** $4i + 7i$
- **b** $7r + 2r$
- **c** $3u + u$
- **d** $7t - 3t$
- **e** $4n - 3n$
- **f** $15t - 10t$

22

4 Simplify these expressions.

   a $3h + 2h + 4h$ **b** $6y + y + 8y$ **c** $m + 5m + 2m$
   d $9p - 5p + 2p$ **e** $8u + 7u - 3u$ **f** $6k - k - 2k$

5 Simplify these expressions.

   a $6d + 4d + 3$ **b** $7 + 3i + 2i$ **c** $10y - 2y + 9$
   d $4p + 2p - 1$ **e** $7 + 7d - 2d$ **f** $6t - 2t + 5u$
   g $9w - 3w + x$ **h** $c + 2c - d$ **i** $5e - e - 4f$

6 Simplify these expressions.

   a $4q + 3q + 6i + i$ **b** $8z + 3z + 4b + 2b$
   c $9u - 3u + 2v + 4v$ **d** $7j - 5j + 3k + 2k$
   e $9m - 5m + 8n - 7n$ **f** $4d + 6d + 9 - 4$

Practice
5C Using algebra and shapes

1   **i**   Write down the perimeter of each rectangle as simply as possible.
    ii   Write down the area of each rectangle as simply as possible.

   a rectangle with width x cm and height 3 cm
   b rectangle with width m cm and height r cm
   c rectangle with width $2p$ cm and height 5 cm

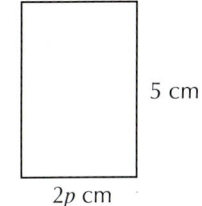

2 Write down the perimeter of each shape as simply as possible.

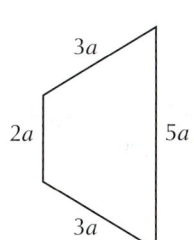

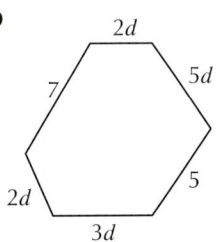

   a trapezium with sides $3a$, $5a$, $3a$, $2a$
   b hexagon with sides $2d$, $5d$, 5, $3d$, $2d$, 7
   c shape with sides t, $5t$, $2t$, $5t$, t, $4t$ (and two inner segments)

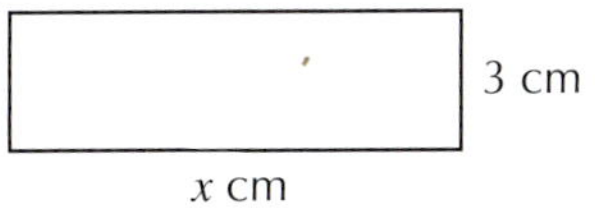

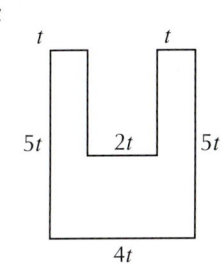

3 Write down the area of each shape as simply as possible.

   a composite shape with labels m, 3, 5, n
   b composite shape with labels a, 9, 5, a

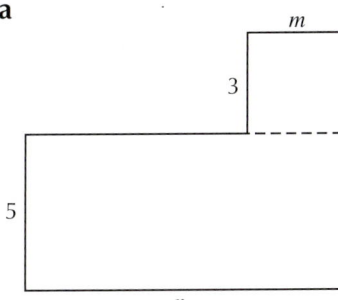

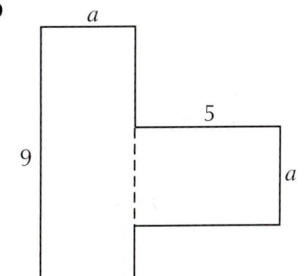

4 Choose one or more of the weights on the right that, together, will balance the weight on the left.

a
$3x + 5$ — $2x - 1$, $x + 2$, $x + 4$, $2x + 3$

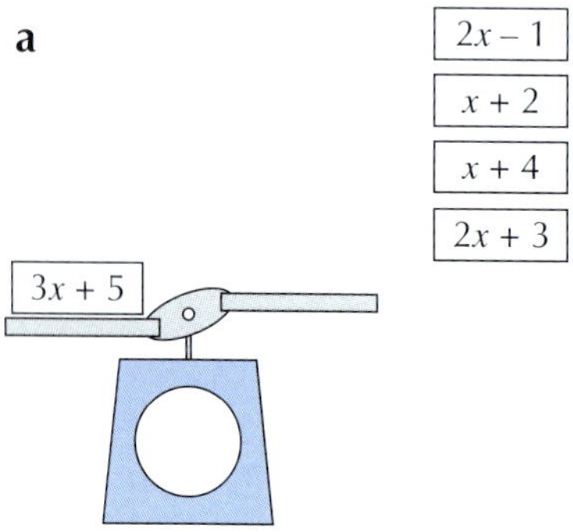

b 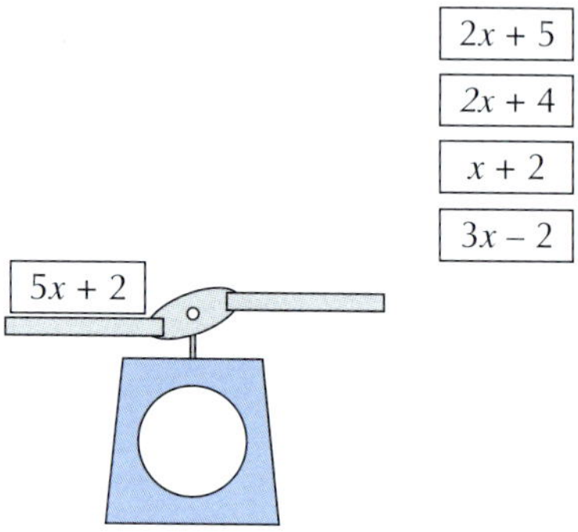
$5x + 2$ — $2x + 5$, $2x + 4$, $x + 2$, $3x - 2$

5D Expanding brackets

1 Expand these brackets.

a $2(4 + 7)$ b $5(9 - 4)$ c $4(a + 3)$
d $3(d + r)$ e $2(3 - s)$ f $4(b - 3)$
g $5(2s + 3)$ h $6(4 + 3i)$ i $3(3u - 1)$
j $6(4 - 5n)$

2 Expand and simplify these expressions.

a $6f + 4(f + 2)$ b $2k + 3(k + 2)$ c $4x + 2(2 + x)$
d $3(m + 5) + 4m$ e $5b + 2(3b + 1)$ f $4(2g + 3) + g$

3 Expand and simplify these expressions.

a $3(b + 2) - 4$ b $3s + 4(s - 4)$ c $5y + 2(3y - 1)$
d $t + 2(t - u)$ e $4n + 2(2n - m)$ f $3(2r - 3n) + 2r$

5E Powers

1 Write these expressions as powers (using index form).

a $4 \times 4 \times 4$ b $3 \times 3 \times 3 \times 3 \times 3 \times 3$ c $10 \times 10 \times 10 \times 10 \times 10$

2 Calculate these powers.

a 2^4 b 3^3 c 2^7 d 4^3 e 10^4

3 Write these expressions as powers (using index form).

a $a \times a \times a$ b $g \times g \times g \times g \times g \times g$
c $S \times S \times S \times S \times S \times S \times S \times S \times S \times S \times S$ d $K \times K$

4 Simplify these expressions.

  a $9 \times k \times k$ **b** $4 \times a \times a \times a$ **c** $5s \times s \times s \times s$
  d $u \times u \times u \times 3$ **e** $4 \times 5 \times t \times t \times t$ **f** $r \times 4r$
  g $3m \times 2m$ **h** $5w \times w \times 2w$ **i** $2j \times 2j \times 2j$

5 Write these expressions as briefly as possible.

  a $m + m + m + m + m + m + m + m$ **b** $t \times t \times t \times t \times t$

6 Show the difference between $6w$ and w^6. Write out each in full.
$6w =$
$w^6 =$

CHAPTER 6 Shape, Space and Measures 2

Practice

6A Perimeter and area of rectangles

1 **i** Calculate the perimeter of each rectangle.
   ii Calculate the area of each rectangle.

  a 9 cm, 7 cm

  b 6 mm, 12 mm

  c 18 m, 11 m

  d 6 cm, 1.6 cm

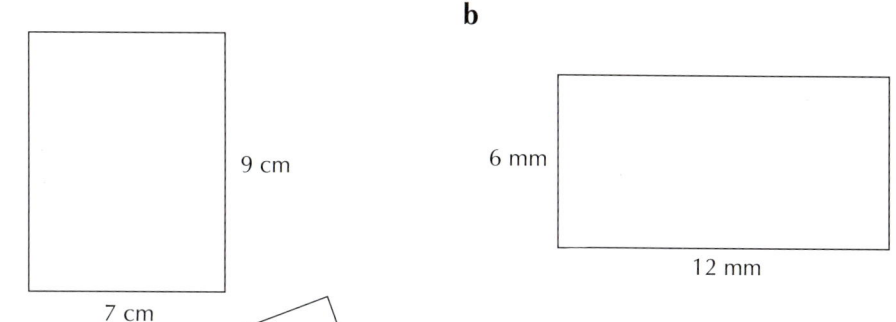

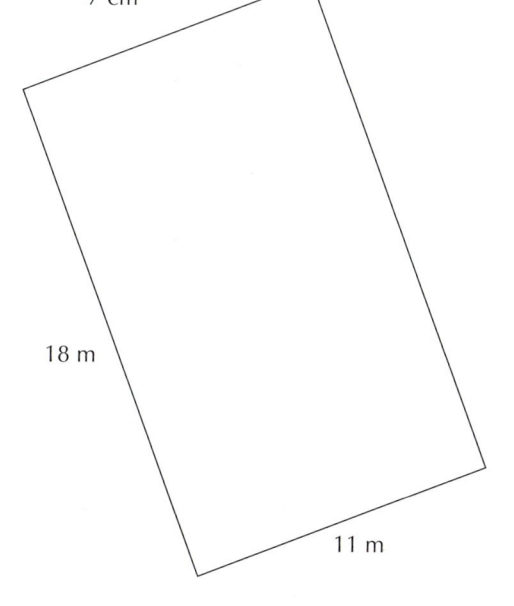

2 **i** Measure the sides of each rectangle to the nearest centimetre.
  ii Calculate the perimeter of each rectangle.
  iii Calculate the area of each rectangle.

a

b

c

3 This diagram shows the ground floor plan of a house.

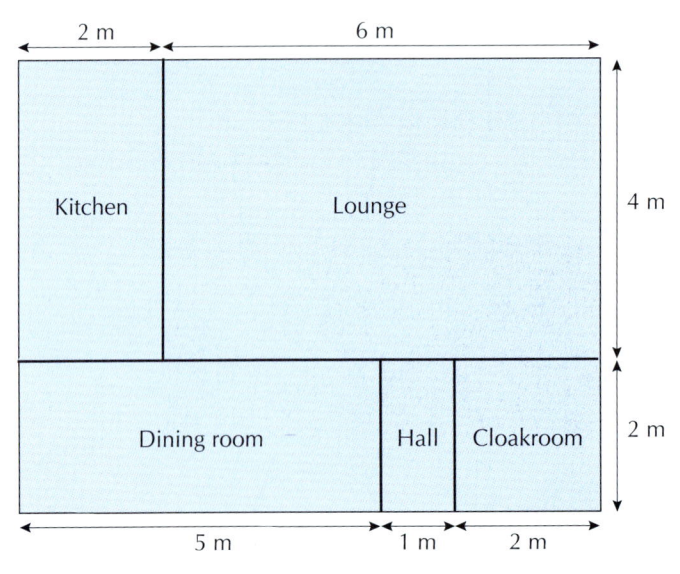

a Calculate the perimeter of each room, including the hall.
b Calculate the area of each room, including the hall.

4 Use centimetre-squared paper to draw three rectangles, each with area 24 cm^2.

Practice
6B Perimeter and area of compound shapes

1 Split each compound shape into rectangles.
Find **i** the perimeter and **ii** the area of each shape.

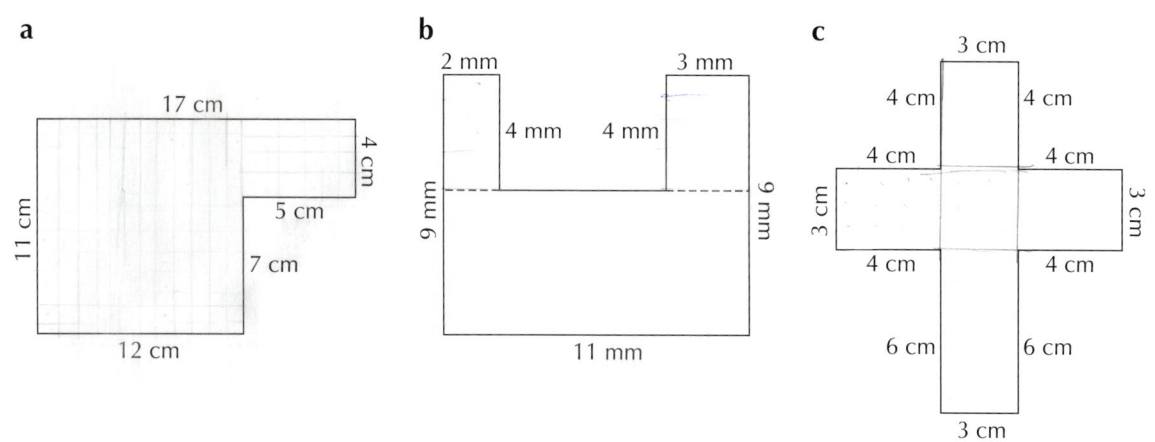

a
- 17 cm (top)
- 11 cm (left)
- 4 cm
- 5 cm
- 7 cm
- 12 cm (bottom)

b
- 2 mm, 3 mm (top)
- 4 mm, 4 mm
- 9 mm (left), 9 mm (right)
- 11 mm (bottom)

c
- 3 cm (top)
- 4 cm, 4 cm
- 4 cm, 4 cm
- 3 cm (left), 3 cm (right)
- 4 cm, 4 cm
- 6 cm, 6 cm
- 3 cm (bottom)

2 Copy each compound shape and find its missing sides.
Find **i** the perimeter and **ii** the area of each shape.

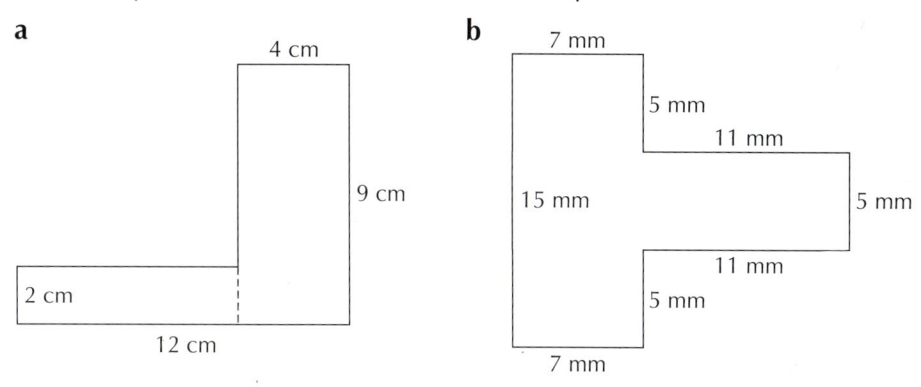

a
- 4 cm (top)
- 9 cm
- 2 cm
- 12 cm (bottom)

b
- 7 mm (top)
- 5 mm
- 11 mm
- 15 mm, 5 mm (right)
- 11 mm
- 5 mm
- 7 mm (bottom)

3 This diagram shows a piece of modern art.

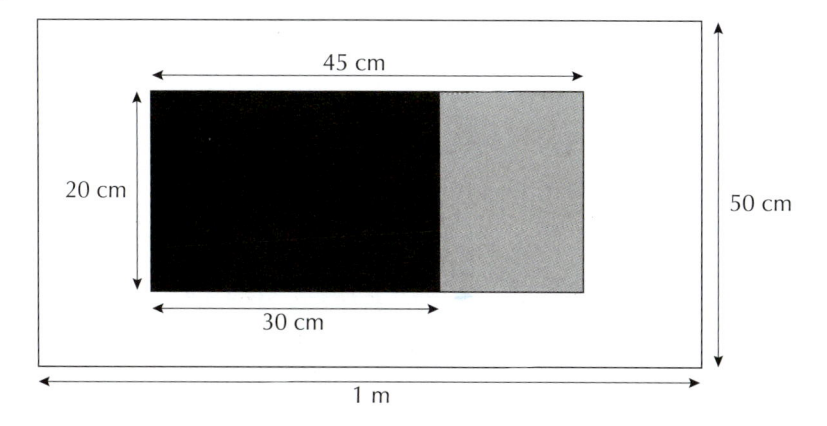

- 45 cm
- 20 cm
- 50 cm
- 30 cm
- 1 m

a Calculate the area that is black.
b Calculate the area that is grey.
c Calculate the area that is white.

27

6 Practice
6C Reading scales

1 **i** Calculate the size of each division on these number lines.
   ii Write down the number to which each arrow is pointing.

   a number line from 0 to 25

   b number line from 0 to 20

   c number line from 0 to 6

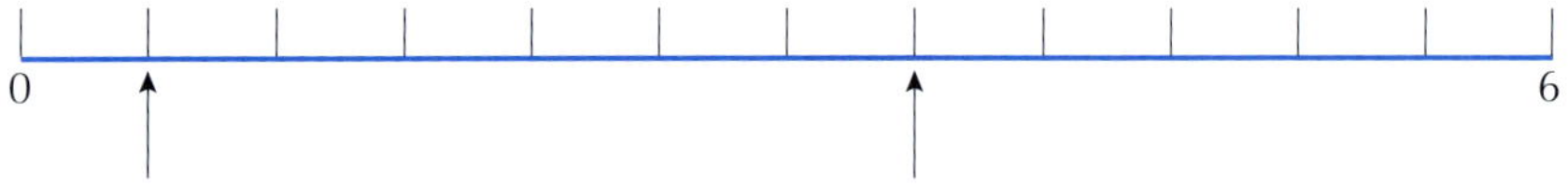

2 Measure the length of each object **i** in millimetres and **ii** in centimetres.

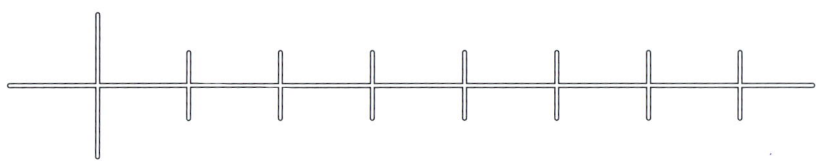

   a arrow

   b rake

   c key

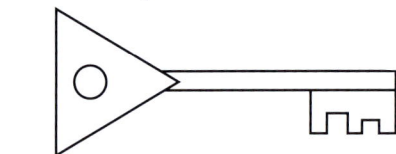

3 Write down the weight shown on each spring balance.

   a scale in grams (0 to 40)

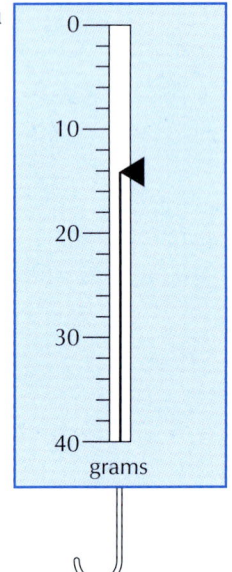

   b scale in kg and g (0 to 3 kg / 0 to 3000 g)

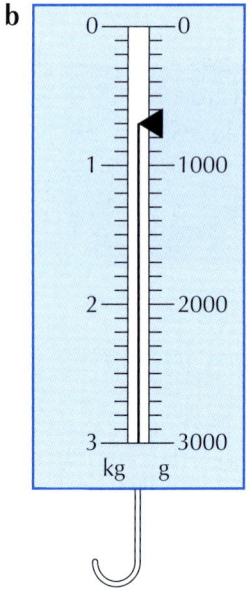

   c scale in grams (0 to 1000)

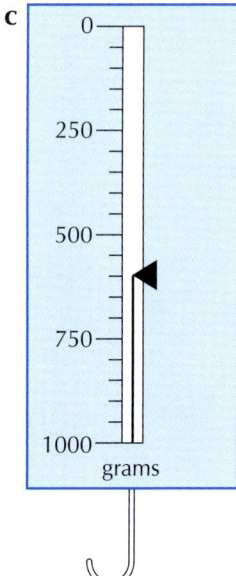

4 The scale shows the heights of different towns above sea level.
A negative height means the town is below sea level.

   a Make a table to show the heights of the towns.
   b Which town is 60 m lower than 220 m?
   c Which town is 40 m lower than −20 m?
   d Which town is 100 m higher than −280 m?

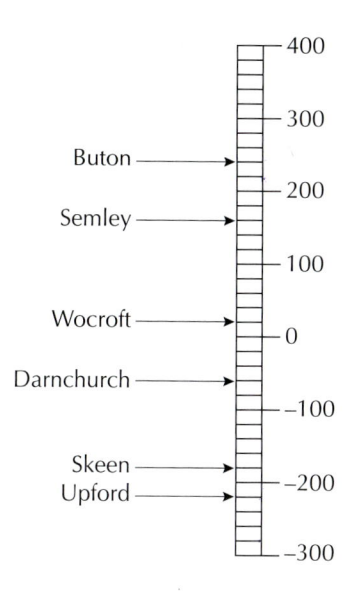

Practice

6D Surface area of cubes and cuboids

1 Find the surface area of each cuboid.

   a 8 cm, 5 cm, 4 cm
   b 5 m, 12 m, 7 m
   c 3 mm, 10 mm, 20 mm

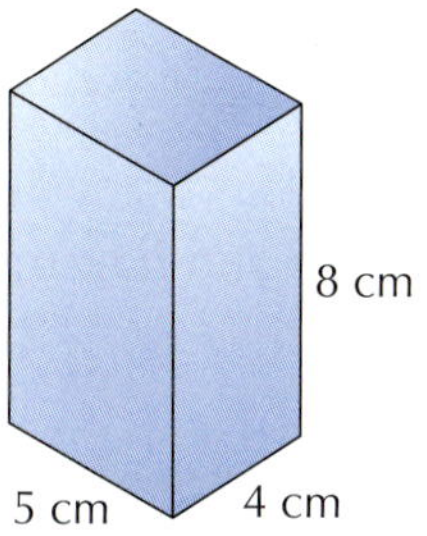

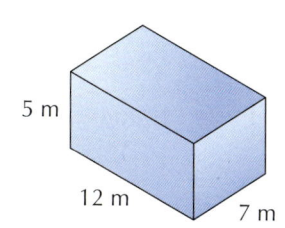

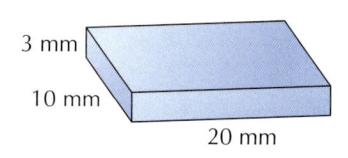

2 Find the surface area of cubes with these edge lengths.

   a 3 cm   **b** 6 cm   **c** 12 cm

3 Calculate the total surface area of the inside and outside of this wardrobe, including the door (ignore the thickness of wood).

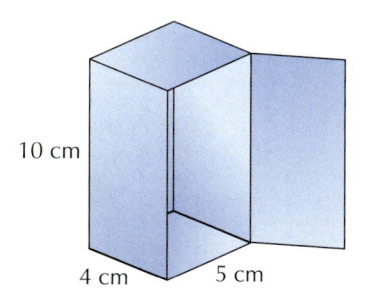

10 cm, 4 cm, 5 cm

4 **a** Use an isometric grid to draw different shapes using four 1-cm cubes. Find the shapes with the greatest surface area.
   b Repeat part **a** using 5 cubes, and then using 6 cubes.
   c Describe how cubes should be arranged to give a solid with the greatest surface area.

6E Converting one metric unit to another

Practice

1 Change each of these lengths to millimetres.
   a 8 cm
   b 2.4 cm
   c 0.7 cm
   d 11.3 cm

2 Change each of these lengths to centimetres.
   a 40 mm
   b 25 mm
   c 72 mm
   d 160 mm
   e 243 mm
   f 6 mm

3 Change each of these lengths to centimetres.
   a 4 m
   b 1.5 m
   c 7.3 m
   d 0.6 m
   e 0.14 m
   f 0.03 m

4 Change each of these lengths to metres.
   a 800 cm
   b 450 cm
   c 223 cm
   d 76 cm
   e 6 cm

5 Change each of these lengths to metres.
   a 9 km
   b 6.4 km
   c 0.8 km
   d 2.156 km
   e 0.06 km

6 Change each of these lengths to kilometres.
   a 7000 m
   b 9500 m
   c 2300 m
   d 300 m
   e 70 m

7 Change each of these capacities **i** to centilitres and **ii** to millilitres.
   a 3 l
   b 5.5 l
   c 0.8 l
   d 9.3 l

8 Change each of these capacities to litres.
   a 6000 ml
   b 200 cl
   c 90 cl
   d 4500 ml
   e 6 cl

9 Work out each of these, giving your answers **i** in the smaller unit and **ii** in the larger unit.
   a 9 mm + 3 cm
   b 3 km + 1300 m
   c 370 cl − 1.6 l
   d 3.4 m − 74 cm
   e 980 g + 1.5 kg
   f 9.3 cm − 17 mm

10 A shopkeeper sells different coloured ribbon by the length.
This diagram shows how much ribbon is left on each reel.

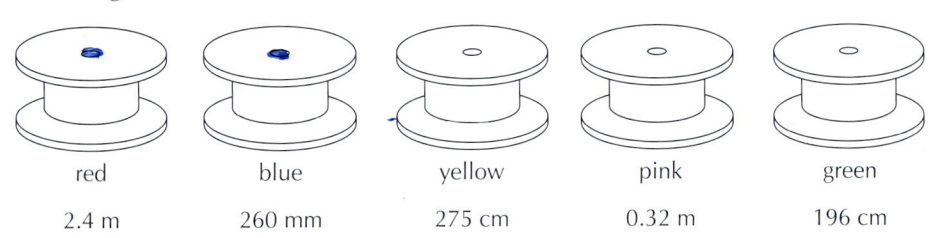

red	blue	yellow	pink	green
2.4 m	260 mm	275 cm	0.32 m	196 cm

   a Arrange the lengths in order, from shortest to longest.
      Hint: Change all lengths to centimetres first.
   b The shopkeeper orders a new reel when there is less than 2 m left.
      Which colours does she need to order?

CHAPTER 7 Algebra 3

Practice 7A Functions

1 a Copy this mapping diagram.

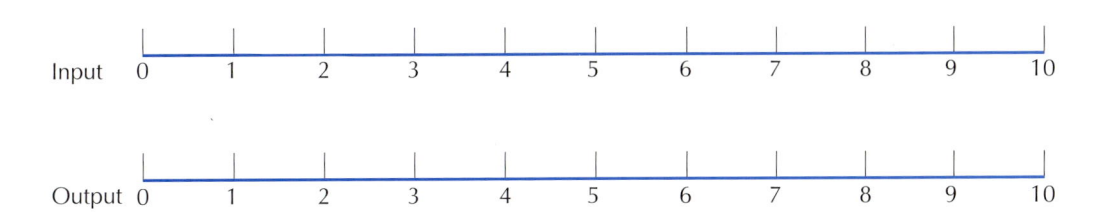

Input 0 1 2 3 4 5 6 7 8 9 10

Output 0 1 2 3 4 5 6 7 8 9 10

    b Map the integer values from 3 to 10 for the function → subtract 3 →.
    c On your diagram, map these input values.
       i 5.5   **ii** 8.5   **iii** 4.5   **iv** 3.5

2 a For each of these functions, use two number lines from 0 to 15 to draw a mapping diagram.
      i → multiply by 2 →   **ii** → add 4 →   **iii** → divide by 2 →
    b On diagrams **i** and **ii**, map the values 3.5, 0.5 and 7.5.

3 a Use two number lines from 0 to 10 to draw a mapping diagram for each of these functions.
      i → multiply by 2 → add 1 →
      ii → subtract 1 → multiply by 2 →
      iii → divide by 2 → add 3 →
    b On diagrams **i** and **ii**, map the values 3.5, 1.5 and 4.5.

Practice 7B Finding functions

1 Find the function that maps these inputs to the outputs.
Each function is either → add → or → subtract →.
    a {1, 2, 3, 4} → {7, 8, 9, 10} + 6
    b {3, 4, 5, 6} → {1, 2, 3, 4} − 2
    c {0, 2, 4, 6} → {5, 7, 9, 11} + 5
    d {10, 15, 20, 25} → {0, 5, 10, 15} − 10

31

2 Find the function that maps these inputs to the outputs.

Each function is either → [multiply] → or → [divide] →.

  a {1, 2, 3, 4} → {5, 10, 15, 20}
  b {4, 8, 12, 16} → {2, 4, 6, 8}
  c {0, 10, 20, 30} → {0, 1, 2, 3}
  d {0, 3, 5, 7} → {0, 9, 15, 21}

3 Find the function that maps these inputs to the outputs.

  a {1, 2, 3, 4} → {0, 1, 2, 3}
  b {5, 6, 7, 8} → {15, 18, 21, 24}
  c {6, 8, 10, 12} → {2, 4, 6, 8}
  d {6, 9, 12, 15} → {2, 3, 4, 5}
  e {3, 8} → {8, 13}
  f {4, 7} → {24, 42}

4 Write down two different functions that map the input 2 to the output 10.

7C Graphs of functions

1 Write these functions starting $y =$

Example → [add 3] →

Answer $y = x + 3$

  a → [subtract 2] →
  b → [multiply by 4] →
  c → [add 7] →
  d → [multiply by 3] →
  e → [subtract 10] →
  f → [divide by 2] →

2 a Copy and complete this table for the function $y = x + 5$.

x	0	1	2	3	4	5
$y = x + 5$						

  b Draw a grid with its x-axis from 0 to 5 and y-axis from 0 to 10.
  c Draw the graph of the function $y = x + 5$.

3 a Copy and complete this table for the function $y = x - 3$.

x	0	1	2	3	4	5	6
$y = x - 3$							

  b Draw a grid with its x-axis from 0 to 6 and y-axis from −5 to 5.
  c Draw the graph of the function $y = x - 3$.

4 a Copy and complete this table for each of the functions.

x	0	1	2	3	4	5
y = x						
y = 2x						
y = 3x						
y = 4x						

  b Draw a grid with its x-axis from 0 to 5 and y-axis from 0 to 20.
  c Draw the graph of each function in the table using the same grid.
  d What is different about the lines?
  e Use a dotted line to sketch the graph of y = 2.5x.

Practice

7D Rules with coordinates

For each question, answer parts **a** to **f** and then answer any additional parts.

a Draw a grid with its x-axis from 0 to 15 and y-axis from 0 to 15.
b Plot the two points and join them with a straight line.
c Mark the points where the coordinates are both whole numbers; write down coordinates, in order.
d Describe the rule for the x-coordinates.
e Describe the rule for the y-coordinates.
f Write down the coordinates of the next three points where the line crosses an intersection.

One example has been done for you.

Example (0, 1) and (4, 11)

  g Does the line pass through the point (16, 42)?
  h What is the y-coordinate when the x-coordinate is 20?

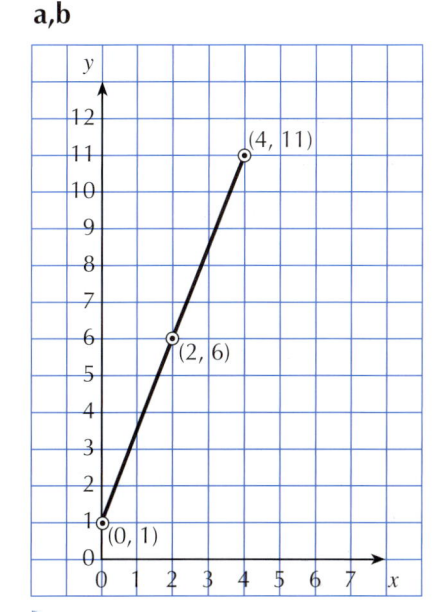

Answer
a,b

c Whole number coordinates, from left to right are (0, 1), (2, 6) and (4, 11).
d The x-coordinates increase by steps of 2 (even numbers).
e The y-coordinates increase by steps of 5.
f The next three points are (6, 16), (8, 21) and (10, 26).
g No, because: three more steps of 2 gives the x-coordinate 10 + 6 = 16 BUT three more steps of 5 gives the y-coordinate 26 + 15 = 41.
h 10 steps of 2 gives the x-coordinate as 20. 10 steps of 5 gives the y-coordinate as 1 + 50 = 51.

1 (0, 0) and (8, 12)
  g What is the y-coordinate when the x-coordinate is 20?

2 (0, 0) and (12, 9)
  g What is the x-coordinate when the y-coordinate is 27?

3 (0, 0) and (4, 12)
  g What is the relationship between the x- and y-coordinates?

4 (0, 12) and (9, 0)
  g What is the y-coordinate when the x-coordinate is −40?

5 (0, 0) and (9, 12)
  g What is the x-coordinate when the y-coordinate is 40?

6 (3, 1) and (12, 7)
  g What is the y-coordinate when the x-coordinate is 51?

7 (0, 12) and (10, 6)
  g What is the y-coordinate when the x-coordinate is 50?

Practice

7E Distance–time graphs

1 Mrs Jay had to travel to a job interview at Penford 120 miles away.
She caught the 0900 train from Shobton and travelled to Deely, 30 miles away. This train journey took one hour.
There she had to wait 30 minutes for a connecting train to Penford. This train took $1\frac{1}{2}$ hours.
Her job interview at Penford lasted 2 hours.
Her return journey to Shobton lasted $1\frac{1}{2}$ hours.

  a Copy this grid, using 2 cm to 1 hour and 1 cm to 10 miles.

Mrs Jay's journey for a job interview

  b Draw on the grid a distance–time graph for Mrs Jay's journey.
  c Mark Deely on the vertical axis.
  d How far was Mrs Jay from Shobton at 1130?
  e At which times was Mrs Jay 60 miles from Shobton?

2 A petrol tanker made this journey along a motorway.
- Filled up at petrol depot.
- Drove 10 miles in 30 minutes to Dibley Sevices.
  Spent 30 minutes filling the pumps.
- Drove a further 20 miles in 1 hour to Penton Sevices.
  Spent 30 minutes filling the pumps and 30 minutes for a tea break.
- Drove a further 30 miles in 1 hour to Hillview Sevices.
  Spent 30 minutes filling the pumps.
- Returned to the depot in 90 minutes.

a Draw a grid with the following scales:
Horizontal axis (time), from 0 to 6 hours, 1 cm to 30 minutes
Vertical axis (distance), from 0 to 60 miles, 1 cm to 5 miles
b Draw on the grid a distance–time graph for the journey.
Mark the places of delivery on the vertical axis.
c How far was the tanker from the depot after
  i 90 minutes? **ii** 3.5 hours? **iii** 5 hours?

CHAPTER 8 Number 3

Practice

8A Rounding

Do not use your calculator.

1 Round these numbers to 1 decimal place.

  a 8.265   **b** 6.849   **c** 3.965
  d 0.095   **e** 4.994   **f** 0.047

2 Round these numbers **i** to the nearest whole number and **ii** to 1 decimal place.

  a 7.32   **b** 8.75   **c** 3.04
  d 19.58   **e** 0.749   **f** 9.955

3 Multiply each of these numbers **i** by 10 **ii** by 1000 and **iii** by 100.

  a 2.7   **b** 0.05   **c** 38   **d** 0.008

4 Divide each of these numbers **i** by 10 **ii** by 1000 and **iii** by 100.

  a 730   **b** 4   **c** 2.8   **d** 35 842

5 Calculate these.

  a 7.4 × 1000   **b** 13 × 100 000
  c 0.87 ÷ 1000   **d** 17.4 ÷ 100
  e 0.0065 × 1000   **f** 19.4 ÷ 10 000

6 Work your way along this chain of calculations for each of these starting numbers.

　　a　2000　　　　　　b　7　　　　　　　　c　0.06

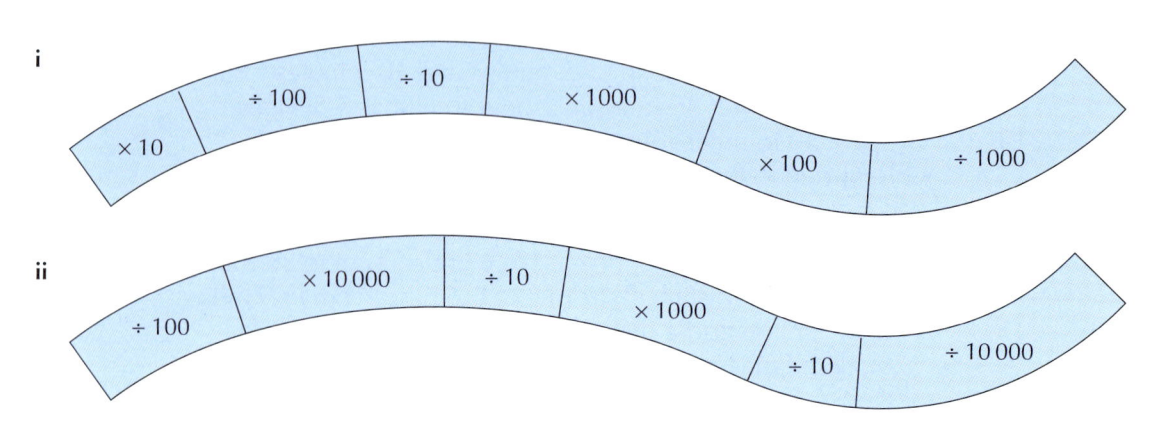

i × 10 → ÷ 100 → ÷ 10 → × 1000 → × 100 → ÷ 1000

ii ÷ 100 → × 10 000 → ÷ 10 → × 1000 → ÷ 10 → ÷ 10 000

Practice

8B Powers of 10

1 Write these numbers in words.

　　a　956 348　　b　15 230 421　　c　8 002 040　　d　604 500 002

2 Write these numbers using figures.

　　a　Ninety-two thousand and fifty-six
　　b　Two hundred and six thousand, one hundred and seven
　　c　Five million, thirty-two thousand and eight

3 This graph shows the numbers of oil shares sold every hour during a trading day.

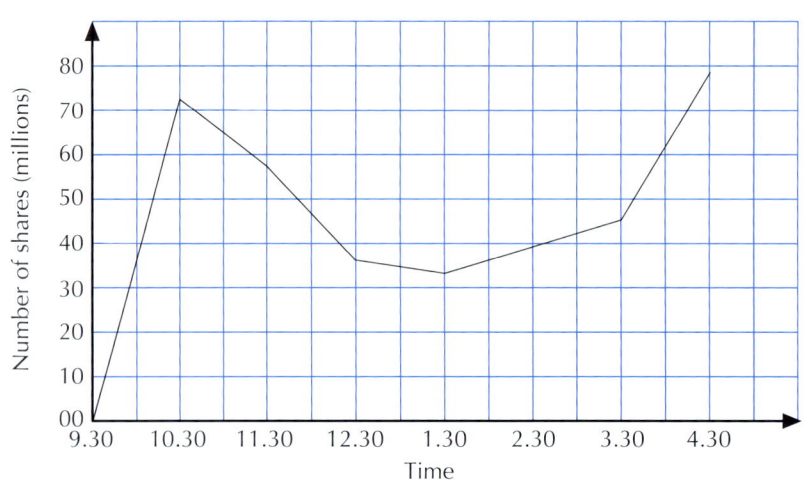

Estimate the number sold each hour. Make a table for your answers.

4 Round these numbers to the nearest **i** thousand **ii** ten thousand **iii** million.

　　a　7 247 964　　b　1 952 599　　c　645 491　　d　9 595 902

5 This table shows the top coal producers in 1996.

Country	Coal production (tons)
USA	948 965 640
India	303 133 600
Russia	250 971 000
Australia	246 050 000
Germany	231 385 420

a i Calculate the total production of these countries.
  ii What is the total production of these countries, to the nearest million?
b i Round each number to the nearest million. Make a new table for your results.
  ii Calculate the total for your table.
c Compare the two totals you have calculated. Why are they different? Which is the more accurate? Which is easier to read?

Practice
8C Estimations

1 Explain why these calculations must be wrong.

  a $53 \times 21 = 1111$
  b $58 \times 34 = 2972$
  c $904 \div 14 = 36$

2 Estimate answers to each of these problems.

  a $6832 - 496$
  b 28×123
  c $521 \div 18$
  d 770×770
  e $\dfrac{58.9 + 36.4}{22.5}$

3 Which is the best estimate for 15.4×21.6?

  a 16×22
  b 15×21
  c 15×22
  d 16×21

4 a Football socks cost £3.71 a pair. Without working out the correct answer, could Ian buy 5 pairs using a £20 note? Explain your answer.
  b Shoelaces cost 68p a pair. The shopkeeper charged Ian £3.25 for 5 pairs. Without working out the correct answer, explain why is this incorrect.

5 Estimate the number to which each arrow is pointing.

  a (number line from 5 to 10)
  b (number line from 3.2 to 5.2)
  c (number line from −10 to 10)

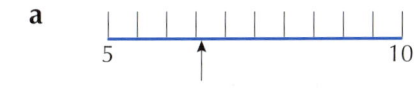

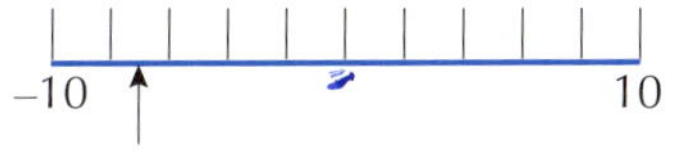

6 Estimate answers to these.

    a 33×777 **b** $274 \div 53$ **c** $\dfrac{34.9 + 73.8}{62.8 - 38.9}$

    d $\frac{1}{5}$ of 973   **e** 7.57^2 **f** 71% of £589

Practice — 8D Adding and subtracting decimals

Do not use a calculator. Show your working.

1 Calculate these.

    a $4.76 + 8.39$ **b** $2.06 + 9.77 + 12.3$
    c $5.28 - 3.75$ **d** $0.87 + 1.79 - 0.94$
    e $78.02 - 23.7 - 19.08$ **f** $9.23 - 2.07 - 1.8$
    g $13 + 91.03 - 2.37$

2 Calculate these. Work in metres.

    a $5\,m - 2.56\,m + 108\,cm$ **b** $0.95\,m + 239\,cm - 1.86\,m$
    c $6\,cm + 0.67\,m - 0.09\,m$ **d** $23\,cm + 0.08\,m - 7\,cm$

3 **a** Calculate the total volume of juice in these full bottles. Work in litres.
      Remember: 1 litre = 100 cl = 1000 ml.

Appley Juice 1.93 l   Sun Orange 37 cl   Cherry Twist 430 ml

    b All the juice is made into a fruit cocktail. Three cups are drunk. If a cup holds 15 cl, how much fruit cocktail is left? Work in litres.

4 The skin is the largest organ in the body and weighs 10.88 kg, on average. The four other largest organs are the liver (1.56 kg), brain (1.41 kg), lungs (1.09 kg) and the heart (0.32 kg).

    a Calculate the total weight of these four organs.
    b How much more does the skin weigh compared to the total weight of the other organs?

5 A candle is 32.7 cm tall. It burns down 18 mm each day.
What is its height at the end of 4 days? Work in centimetres.

Practice

8E Efficient calculations

1 Without using a calculator, work out the value of these.

    a $\dfrac{20-6}{2+5}$ b $\dfrac{7+90}{9-0.4}$

2 Use a calculator to do the calculations in Question 1.
Are your answers the same as before?

3 For each part of Question 2, write down the sequence of keys that you pressed.

4 Work out the value of these. Round your answers to 1 decimal place, if necessary.

    a $\dfrac{689+655}{100-58}$ b $\dfrac{420-78}{54 \div 3}$

    c $\dfrac{36 \times 84}{29+17}$ d $\dfrac{296+112}{183-159}$

5 a Estimate the answer to: $\dfrac{443-178}{53-27}$

   b Now use a calculator to work out the answer correct to 1 decimal place. Is your answer about the same?

6 Calculate these.

    a $\sqrt{344\,569}$ b 5.4^2
    c $\sqrt{50.6+39.65}$ d $(12.3-2.6)^2$

7 a Calculate $\dfrac{387+231}{306 \div 17}$

   b Write your answer to part **a** as a mixed number.

Practice

8F Long multiplication and long division

1 Work out these long multiplication problems. Use any method you are happy with.

    a 13×32 b 54×27 c 19×275 d 148×38

2 Work out these long division problems. Use any method you are happy with. Some of the problems will have a remainder.

    a $420 \div 12$ b $600 \div 22$ c $738 \div 38$ d $884 \div 26$

For Questions 3–6, decide whether these problems are long multiplication or long division. Then do the appropriate calculation, showing your method clearly.

3 A sports stadium has 23 rows of seats. Each row has 84 seats.
How many people can be seated in the stadium?

4 A bag contains 448 g of flour. The flour is used to make cakes. Each cake contains 14 g of flour.

   a How many cakes were made?
   b How much flour is needed to make 234 cakes?

5 Floor tiles measure 35 cm by 26 cm. They cover a floor measuring 945 cm by 660 cm.

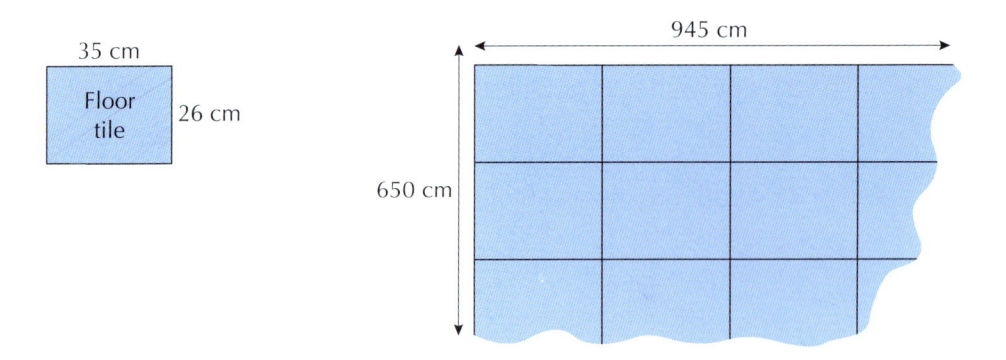

   a How many tiles are next to the long edge of the floor?
   b How many tiles are next to the short edge of the floor?
   c How many tiles were used to cover the floor?

6 An oven can bake 24 pizzas at a time. Each pizza takes 11 minutes to cook.

   a How many pizzas could be baked in 3 hours?
   b How long would it take to bake 540 pizzas, in minutes?
   c Convert your answer to part **b** to hours and minutes.

CHAPTER 9 Shape, Space and Measures 3

Practice

9A Congruent shapes

1 Use your ruler to check which of these triangles are congruent. Write your answer like this, e.g. A = D.

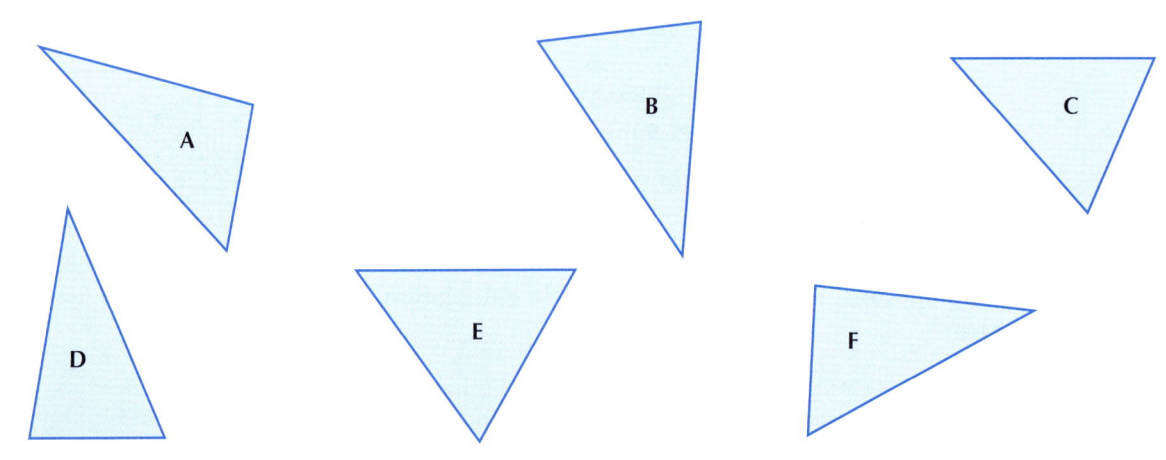

2 Which of these shapes are congruent?
Write your answer like this, e.g. A = D = F.

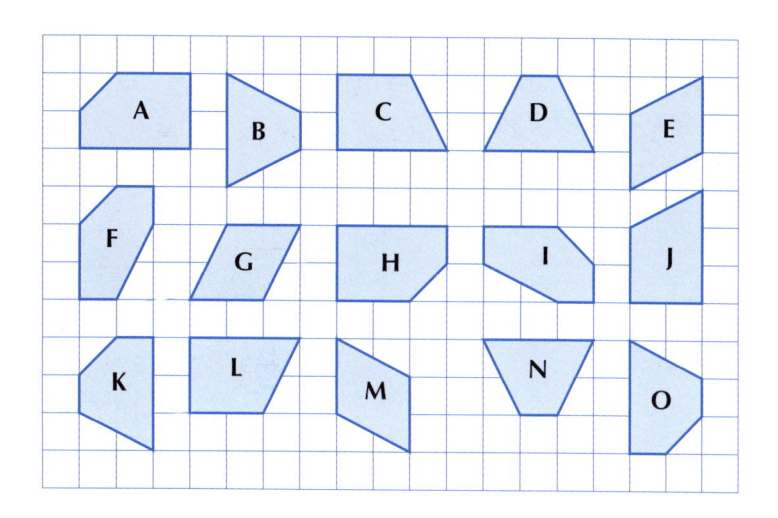

3 a Use triangular dotted paper. Draw 15 shapes by joining some of the dots shown in the diagram. A few examples are shown.
Label your shapes from A to N.

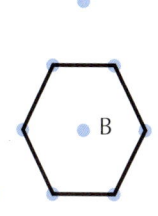

b Write down the shapes that are congruent.

Practice
9B Combinations of transformations

1 a Describe the single transformation that maps
  i   A on to F
  ii D on to A
  iii C on to A
  iv E on to F
  v   D on to B

b Describe the combination of two transformations that maps
  i   A on to D
  ii B on to C
  iii E on to G

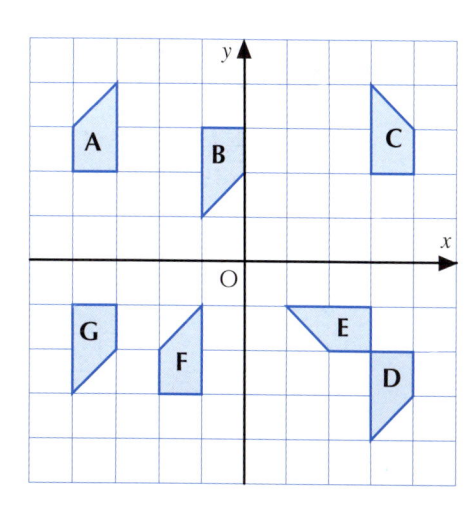

41

2 a Copy this diagram on to square paper.
  b Reflect shape A in the dotted line. Label the image B.
  c Reflect shape B in the *x*-axis. Label the image C.
  d What single transformation maps shape A on to shape C?

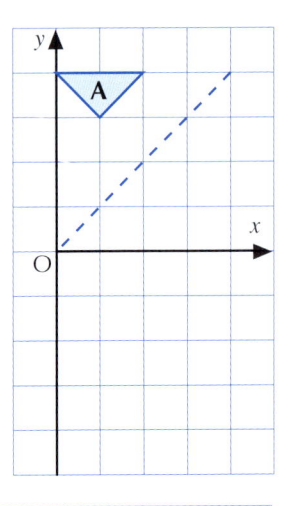

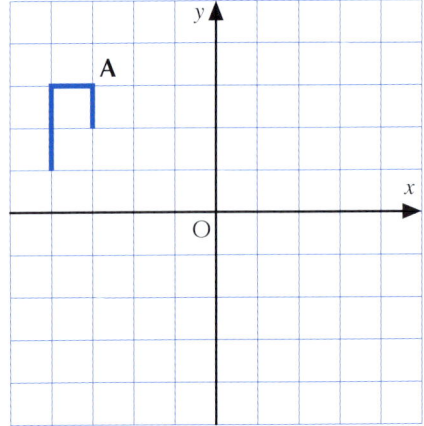

3 a Reflect shape A in the *y*-axis. Label the image B.
  b What combination of two transformations maps shape A on to shape B?

4 a Which single transformation maps any shape on to itself?
  b Describe a combination of two transformations that map any shape on to itself.

9C Enlargements

1 Use squared paper to enlarge each of these shapes. The scale factor is given.

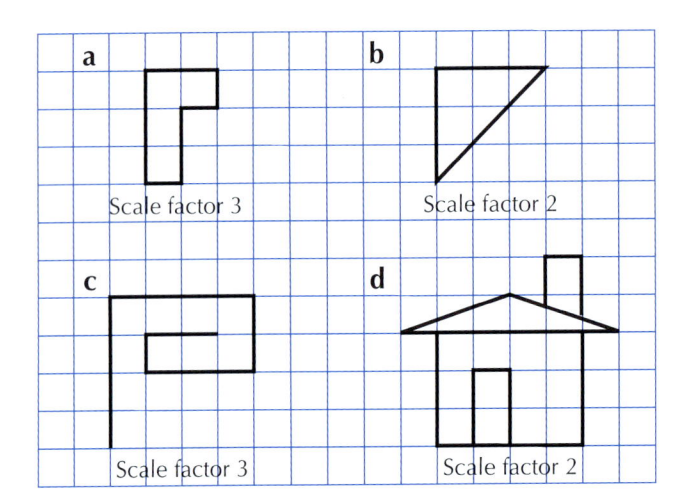

a Scale factor 3
b Scale factor 2
c Scale factor 3
d Scale factor 2

2 Use squared paper to enlarge each of these shapes. The scale factor and centre of enlargement are given.

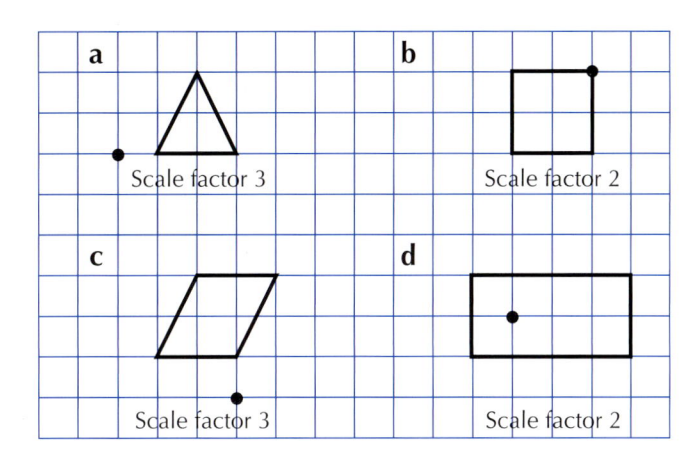

a Scale factor 3
b Scale factor 2
c Scale factor 3
d Scale factor 2

Practice
9D Shape and ratio

Express all ratio answers in their simplest form.

1 Express each of these ratios in its simplest form.

   a 90 cm : 20 cm   **b** 32 mm : 72 mm   **c** 150 cm : 2 m
   d 1.8 cm : 40 mm   **e** 0.65 km : 800 m

2

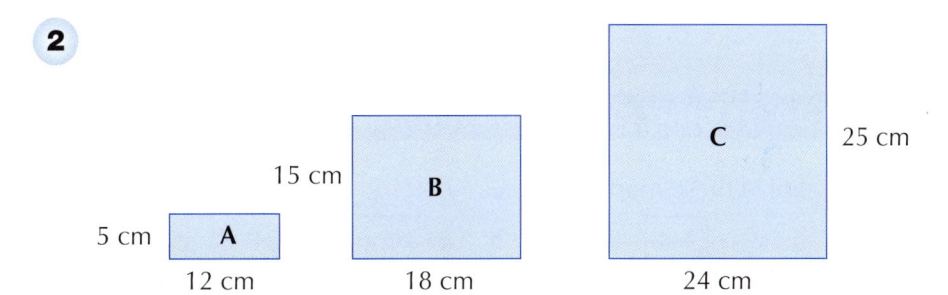

A: 5 cm × 12 cm
B: 15 cm × 18 cm
C: 25 cm × 24 cm

   a Find the ratio of the base of rectangle A to rectangle B.
   b **i** Calculate the areas of rectangles A and B.
      ii Find the ratio of the area of rectangle A to rectangle B.
   c What fraction is area A of area B?
   d **i** Calculate the area of rectangle C.
      ii Find the ratio of the area of rectangle B to rectangle C.

3 This diagram shows the design of a new flag.

   a Calculate the areas of blue and white material.
   b Calculate the ratio of the blue area to the white area.

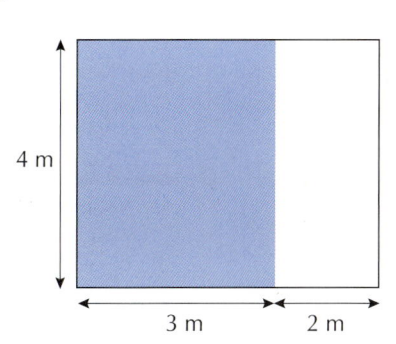

4 m, 3 m, 2 m

4 This diagram shows the plan of a garden.

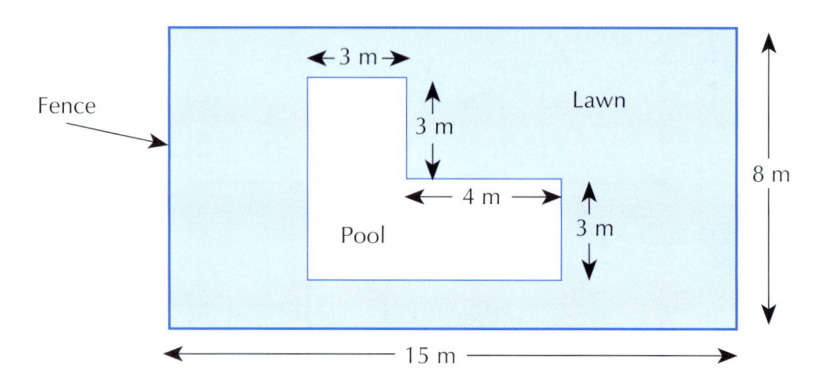

- **a i** Calculate the perimeter of the fence.
  - **ii** Calculate the perimeter of the pool.
  - **iii** Find the ratio of the perimeter of the fence to the perimeter of the pool.
- **b i** Calculate the area of the pool.
  - **ii** Calculate the area of the lawn.
  - **iii** Find the ratio of the lawn area to the pool area.

CHAPTER 10 Algebra 4

Practice

10A Solving equations and mapping

1 Solve these mappings.

- **a** $x \to \boxed{+4} \to 9$
- **b** $a \to \boxed{\times 3} \to 21$
- **c** $m \to \boxed{-6} \to 11$
- **d** $p \to \boxed{\div 3} \to 9$
- **e** $n \to \boxed{-2} \to 25$
- **f** $r \to \boxed{+8} \to 40$

2 Copy and complete these solutions to mappings.

- **a** $x \to \boxed{} \to 9$
  $? \leftarrow \boxed{+5} \leftarrow ?$
  $x =$
- **b** $d \to \boxed{} \to 28$
  $? \leftarrow \boxed{\div 4} \leftarrow ?$
  $d =$
- **c** $n \to \boxed{} \to 6$
  $? \leftarrow \boxed{\times 3} \leftarrow ?$
  $n =$
- **d** $p \to \boxed{} \to 27$
  $19 \leftarrow \boxed{} \leftarrow ?$
  $p =$

3 Solve these equations.
Write each equation as a mapping. Then solve the mapping.

- **a** $c - 2 = 7$
- **b** $4w = 36$
- **c** $q + 13 = 18$
- **d** $6d = 48$
- **e** $\frac{u}{2} = 7$
- **f** $V - 11 = 17$

Practice

10B Equations and mappings involving two operations

1 Solve these mappings.

a $m \to \boxed{\times 2} \to \boxed{+4} \to 10$
b $d \to \boxed{\times 4} \to \boxed{-7} \to 13$

c $k \to \boxed{\times 9} \to \boxed{+7} \to 25$
d $t \to \boxed{\times 4} \to \boxed{-16} \to 20$

e $e \to \boxed{\times 3} \to \boxed{-11} \to 1$
f $r \to \boxed{\times 5} \to \boxed{-32} \to 23$

2 Copy and complete these solutions to mappings.

a $b \to \boxed{} \to \boxed{-4} \to 11$
$? \leftarrow \boxed{+5} \leftarrow \boxed{} \leftarrow ?$
$b =$

b $s \to \boxed{\times 4} \to \boxed{} \to 18$
$? \leftarrow \boxed{} \leftarrow \boxed{-6} \leftarrow ?$
$s =$

c $f \to \boxed{} \to \boxed{-4} \to 6$
$5 \leftarrow \boxed{} \leftarrow \boxed{} \leftarrow ?$
$f =$

3 Write a mapping for each problem. Then solve the mapping.

a If I multiply my number by *n* by 6 then subtract 5, the answer is 19. What is *n*?

b If I multiply my number by *n* by 4 then subtract *y*, the answer is 3. What is *n*?

c If I multiply my number by *n* by 5 then add 13, the answer is 48. What is *n*?

d If I multiply my number by *n* by 12 then add 9, the answer is 45. What is *n*?

4 To solve these equations, write each equation as a mapping. Then solve the mapping.

a $4x + 3 = 15$
b $5y - 4 = 6$
c $2t - 13 = 5$
d $6p + 7 = 31$
e $9k + 3 = 21$
f $10r - 16 = 24$

Practice

10C Substitution into expressions

1 Write down the value of each expression for each value of *x*.

a $4x$ when
   i $x = 2$ ii $x = 7$ iii $x = -3$

b $p + 2$ when
   i $p = 4$ ii $p = 0$ iii $p = -10$

c $4d + 3$ when
   i $d = 2$ ii $d = 6$ iii $d = 20$

45

d 2s – 3 when
      i   s = 3   ii s = 10   iii s = 50
   e $\frac{m}{3}$ when
      i   m = 6   ii m = 30   iii m = –24
   f 3n – 2 when
      i   n = 2   ii n = 0   iii n = 100

2 If p = 3 and q = 5, find the value of each of these.
   a 2q – p   b q + 3p   c 3p – q

3 If r = 2 and s = 3, find the value of each of these.
   a r – s   b r – 2s   c 2r + 3s

4 If x = 3, y = 5 and z = 2 find the value of each of these.
   a xyz   b y + z – x   c xz + y   d 2x + 3y + 4z

Practice
10D Substitution into formulae

1 The cost of a sheet of glass is given by the formula C = 3bh where C is the cost (£), b the breadth and h the height in metres.

Calculate the cost of these sheets of glass:
   a breadth 2 m, height 4 m   b breadth 5 m, height 1 m
   c breadth 4 m, height 2.5 m

2 Given that C = F + 4d, find the value of C when
   a F = 12, d = 6   b F = 20, d = 15   c F = 100, d = 200

3 a The weight, W g of a pack of sausages is given by the formula W = 50n where n is the number of sausages in the pack.
   Calculate the weight of a pack containing
      i   6 saugages   ii 10 sausages   iii 18 sausages.

   b The weight, W g of a barbecue pack of sausages and burgers is given by the formula

   W = 50n + 100m

   where n is the number of sausages and m is the number of burgers in the pack.
   Calculate the weight of a pack when
      i   n = 6, m = 4   ii n = 8, m = 8   iii n = 14, m = 15

4 The average, A, of three numbers m, n and p is given by the formula

$A = \dfrac{m + n + p}{3}$.

Calculate the value of A when
- **a** $m = 4$, $n = 2$, $p = 6$
- **b** $m = 5$, $n = 11$, $p = 11$
- **c** $m = 15$, $n = 15$, $p = 45$

5 The approximate area of a circle of radius r is given by the formula

$A = 3 \times r \times r$

where A is the area and r is the radius.

Find the area of a circle of radius
- **a** 5 cm
- **b** 9 cm
- **c** 20 cm.

Practice

10E Creating your own expressions

1 Write an expression for each of these using the letters suggested.
- **a** The sum of the numbers d and 3
- **b** The number u reduced by 5
- **c** The product of the numbers w, 7 and s
- **d** One third of the number m
- **e** The number of toes on f feet

2
- **a** How many months are there in Y years?
- **b** How many metres are there in x centimetres?

3 Michael is H cm tall now.
- **a** He was 5 cm shorter a year ago. How tall was he then?
- **b** In 3 years time, he will be x cm taller. How tall will he be then?

Michael's taller sister Briony has a height of S cm.
- **c** How much taller is Briony?
- **d** What is the average height of Michael and Briony?

4
- **a** A Chocolate Wheel costs c pence and a Frother costs f pence. What is the total cost of
  - **i** a Chocolate Wheel and a Frother?
  - **ii** 5 Frothers?
  - **iii** 3 Chocolate Wheels and 2 Frothers?
- **b** How much change from a £2 coin would you receive for each of the purchases in part **a**?

CHAPTER 11 Handling Data 2

Practice 11A Statistical surveys

Choose one of the five statements below for your statistical survey.
* Write three or four good questions for your questionnaire
* Make a data recording sheet.
* Collect information from at least 30 people.
* Write a report based on your data.

1. Do girls eat more fruit than boys?

2. Would pupils prefer more English lessons or more Maths lessons?

3. Do Year 7 pupils watch less football than Year 8 pupils?

4. How often do people go to the cinema?

5. Do people think crime has increased in their area?

Practice 11B Stem-and-leaf diagrams

1. The speeds of 35 cars are shown in this stem-and-leaf diagram.

1	0 9 9 9
2	1 2 2 3 4 4 5 6 6 6 8 9
3	0 4 4 5 5 6 6 7 8 8 8 8 9
4	0 3 3 6 8 9

   Key: 4 | 3 means 43 mph

   a What is the mode?
   b Calculate the range.
   c The speed limit is 30mph. How many cars broke the speed limit?

2. The ages of 25 children are shown in this stem-and-leaf diagram.

11	9 9 9 10 11 11
12	0 0 1 2 2 3 4 5 7 10 10 10
13	0 3 3 4 5

   Key: 12 | 4 means 12 yrs 4 months

   Note: Ages are rounded down to the nearest month.

   a How many children are 12 years old?
   b How many children have birthdays in March?
   c Calculate the mode and range.

3 Here are the weights of 27 letters in grams.

48	29	62	48	96	45	30	59	16
88	63	10	74	64	38	90	25	8
44	92	67	78	33	50	23	60	18

a Make a stem-and-leaf diagram for the data. Remember to show the key.
b What is the mode?
c Calculate the range.
d Letters weighing 60 g or more are charged 41p for first class delivery. How many letters need this postage?

Practice
11C Pie charts

1 Draw pie charts to represent the data.

a The numbers of birds spotted on a field trip

Bird	Crow	Thrush	Starling	Magpie
Frequency	8	4	6	2

b The sizes of dresses sold in a shop during one week

Size	8	10	12	14	16	18
Frequency	4	12	10	8	4	2

2 150 children went on one of four school summer holidays.

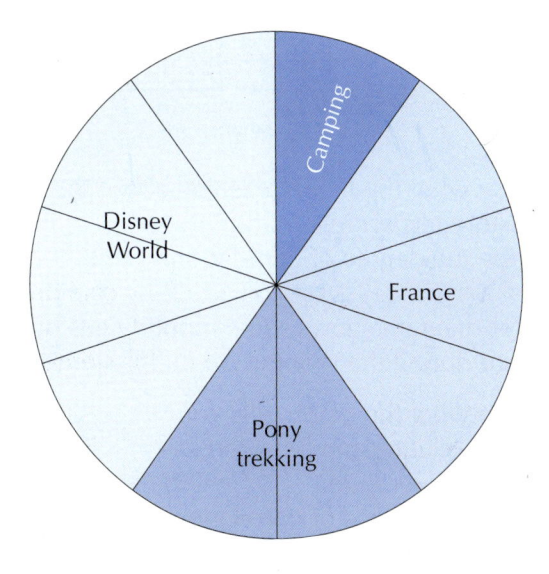

How many children chose these holidays?

a Camping   b France   c Pony trekking   d DisneyWorld

11 Practice 11D Scatter graphs

1 This scatter diagram shows the numbers of newspapers and lottery tickets sold during a day.

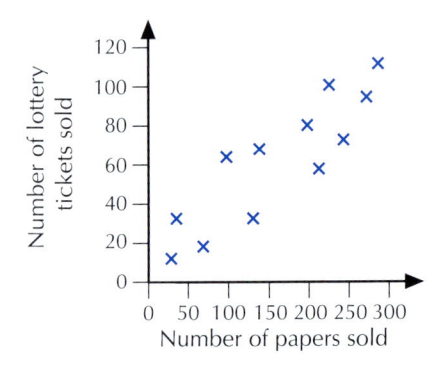

a Describe what the graph tells you about the relationship between the sales of newspapers and lottery tickets.
b Describe the degree of correlation.

2 This scatter diagram shows the heights and history test scores of 20 children.

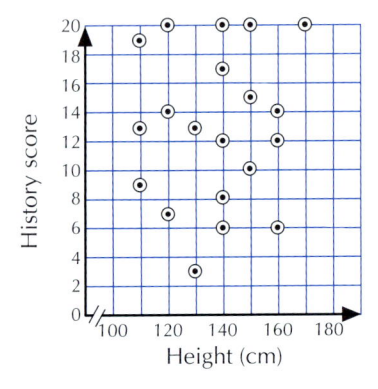

a Describe what the graph tells you about the relationship between height and history test score.
b Describe the degree of correlation.

3 This scatter diagram shows some monthly gas bills and the average temperature during the month.

a Describe what the graph tells you about the relationship between gas bills and temperature.
b Describe the degree of correlation.

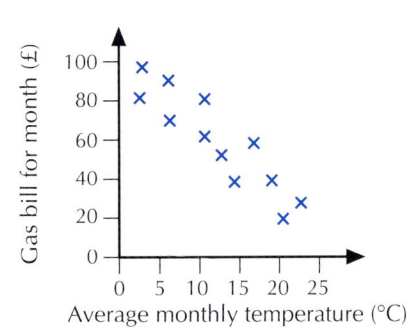

50

4 This table shows the class positions pupils have in their Science and Mathematics classes.

Pupil	Jo	Ken	Lim	Tony	Dee	Sam	Pat	Les	Kay	Val	Rod
Science	24	3	13	21	5	15	22	7	12	27	14
Maths	20	5	10	14	9	15	26	1	16	24	11

a Copy these scatter graph axes and plot the points. The first two points have been done for you.

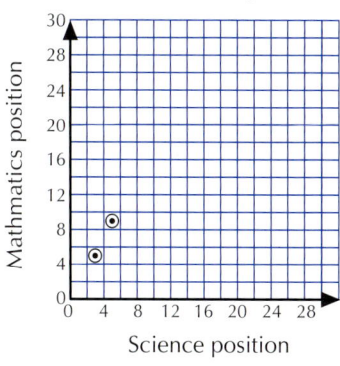

b Describe what your graph tells you about the relationship between pupils' Science and Maths positions in class.

c Which of these best describes the degree of correlation: positive correlation, negative correlation, no correlation?

Practice
11E Analysing data

Do this, for each of the five questions:

* Decide how best to collect the data (questionnaire, experiment, or secondary sources, e.g. books, newspapers).
* Make a data-recording sheet. Collect the data.
* Organise your data into tables, etc.
* Draw diagrams to illustrate your data.
* Make any necessary calculations, e.g. mean, range.
* Write a conclusion.

1 How many times can you catch a ball with your weak hand before dropping it?

2 Do we eat more vegetables now, compared to 10 years ago?

3 How often do people eat from a barbecue?

4 Are the leaves at the bottom of a plant bigger than the leaves in the middle?

5 How long does it take the average person to travel to work?

CHAPTER 12 Number 4

Practice

12A Fractions

1 Copy and complete these.

    a $\frac{9}{4} = \frac{\square}{12}$ **b** $\frac{20}{3} = \frac{180}{\square}$ **c** $\frac{11}{2} = \frac{99}{\square}$

    d $\frac{32}{7} = \frac{\square}{35}$ **e** $\frac{100}{28} = \frac{\square}{7}$ **f** $\frac{144}{60} = \frac{12}{\square}$

2   **a** How many fifths are in $3\frac{4}{5}$?

    b How many thirds are in $7\frac{1}{3}$?

    c How many twelfths are in $4\frac{7}{12}$?

    d How many sevenths are in 9?

3 Convert these mixed numbers to top-heavy fractions.

    a $1\frac{2}{3}$ **b** $3\frac{1}{8}$ **c** $2\frac{5}{6}$

    d $5\frac{1}{4}$ **e** $9\frac{1}{2}$ **f** $6\frac{3}{10}$

4 Convert these decimals to fractions.

    a 0.7   **b** 0.6   **c** 0.45

    d 0.16   **e** 0.08   **f** 0.33

5 Convert each of these top-heavy fractions to a mixed number in its simplest form.

    a $\frac{13}{5}$ **b** $\frac{32}{3}$ **c** $\frac{28}{9}$

    d $\frac{40}{6}$ **e** $\frac{60}{8}$ **f** $\frac{84}{18}$

    g $\frac{133}{21}$ **h** thirteen thirds   **i** eighteen eighths

6 What fraction of a litre are these?

    a 80 cl   **b** 55 cl   **c** 240 cl

    d 700 ml   **e** 245 ml   **f** 3350 ml

Remember: 1 litre = 100 cl and 1 litre = 1000 ml.

Practice

12B Adding and subtracting fractions

If necessary, convert your answers to mixed numbers and cancel.

1 Find the lowest common multiple of these pairs of numbers.

    a 2, 5   **b** 6, 8   **c** 2, 6

    d 10, 15   **e** 9, 12

For Questions 2–4, convert the fractions to equivalent fractions with a common denominator. Then work out the answers. Cancel your answers and write them as mixed numbers if necessary.

2 a $\frac{2}{5} + \frac{1}{2}$ b $\frac{5}{8} + \frac{1}{12}$ c $\frac{5}{6} + \frac{1}{3}$ d $\frac{4}{7} + \frac{3}{5}$

3 a $\frac{3}{5} - \frac{1}{2}$ b $\frac{5}{9} - \frac{1}{6}$ c $\frac{7}{8} - \frac{2}{3}$ d $\frac{7}{10} - \frac{1}{4}$

4 a $\frac{3}{7} + \frac{2}{3}$ b $\frac{5}{12} + \frac{1}{8}$ c $\frac{7}{9} + \frac{5}{6}$

  d $\frac{3}{5} + \frac{1}{2} + \frac{7}{10}$ e $\frac{7}{9} - \frac{1}{2}$ f $\frac{11}{15} - \frac{2}{5}$

  g $\frac{5}{6} - \frac{1}{10}$ h $\frac{2}{3} + \frac{5}{6} - \frac{5}{12}$

Practice
12C BODMAS

Do not use a calculator. Show all of your working.

1 Write down the operation that you would do first in each of these calculations. Then calculate the answer.

  a 12 − 3 × 2 b 2 × (9 − 5) c 10 × 2 ÷ 5 + 3
  d 30 − 20 + 10 e 12 + 8 − 3^2 f 4 × (2 + 5)^2

2 Calculate these. Show each step of your calculation.

  a 3^2 + 5 × 2 b 10 − (1 + 2)^2 c 3 × 12 ÷ 3^2

  d 32 ÷ (3^2 − 1) e $\frac{60 + 12}{2 \times 3}$ f $\frac{60}{(6 + 3^2)}$

  g 1.5 + 3 × (2.4 − 0.8) − 2.1

3 Copy each calculation. Insert brackets to make the answer true.

  a 11 − 7 − 1 + 4 = 1 b 1 + 4 + 3^2 = 50
  c 24 ÷ 2 × 3 = 4 d 6 + 9 ÷ 12 ÷ 4 = 5
  e 12 − 3^2 − 7 × 4 = 4

Practice
12D Multiplying decimals

Do not use a calculator.

1 Calculate these.

  a 0.6 × 0.7 b 0.9 × 0.9 c 0.5 × 0.7 d 0.2 × 0.3
  e 0.4^2 f 0.4 × 0.9 g 0.3 × 0.6 h 0.8 × 0.1

2 Calculate these.

a 0.3×0.04 b 0.09×0.4 c 0.06×0.06 d 0.007×0.2
e 0.08×0.03 f 0.4×0.08 g 0.003×0.2 h 0.9×0.002

3 Calculate these.

a 40×0.7 b 0.4×60 c 20×0.2 d 0.9×90

4 Calculate these.

a 200×0.9 b 0.8×400 c 500×0.09
d 2000×0.7 e 0.08×300 f 9000×0.004
g 70×0.04 h 300×0.002

5 A seed weighs 0.04 g. How much do 600 seeds weigh?

6 Sound travels about 0.3 km in 1 second. How far does sound travel in
a 200 seconds b 600 seconds c 0.1 seconds? Work in kilometres.

Practice
12E Dividing decimals

Do not use a calculator.

1 Calculate these.

a $0.6 \div 0.3$ b $0.8 \div 0.2$ c $0.36 \div 0.2$ d $0.9 \div 0.3$
e $0.4 \div 0.1$ f $0.15 \div 0.3$ g $0.35 \div 0.5$ h $0.08 \div 0.2$

2 Calculate these.

a $9 \div 0.3$ b $40 \div 0.8$ c $60 \div 0.3$ d $48 \div 0.6$
e $500 \div 0.2$ f $900 \div 0.3$ g $5000 \div 0.5$ h $120 \div 0.6$

3 Calculate these.

a $0.8 \div 0.04$ b $0.6 \div 0.02$ c $0.48 \div 0.06$ d $0.16 \div 0.04$

4 Calculate these.

a $30 \div 0.6$ b $600 \div 0.3$ c $20 \div 0.05$
d $3000 \div 0.1$ e $80 \div 0.02$

5 £1 buys 0.05 g of platinum. How much does 4 g of platinum cost?

6 An advertiser pays 0.04p to a website every time it is hit (a hit is when someone visits the website). In 1 month, the website is paid £16 (= 1600p). How many hits did the website receive?

CHAPTER 13 Algebra 5

Practice

13A Expand and simplify

1 Simplify these expressions.
- **a** $4p + 7p$
- **b** $9u - 3u$
- **c** $7d - d$
- **d** $3i + 5i + 8i$
- **e** $4n + 5n - 5n$
- **f** $10h - 7h - h$
- **g** $2f - 7f$
- **h** $-6y - 3y$
- **i** $2d - 5d - 5d$

2 Simplify these expressions.
- **a** $7s + 2s + 4t$
- **b** $9i - 4i + 2j$
- **c** $4a + 3b + 2b$
- **d** $5d + 4y + 3d$
- **e** $6r + 3h - 4r$
- **f** $5b + 3d - 7d$
- **g** $5u + 2a + 3u + 4a$
- **h** $4d + 5y - 2y + 3d$
- **i** $10k + 4p - 7k - 2p$
- **j** $6t - 3g + 2t - 4g$

3 Expand these expressions.
- **a** $4(x + 8)$
- **b** $7(3d - 5)$
- **c** $2(4f + 2e)$
- **d** $d(3 - u)$
- **e** $m(2r + c)$
- **f** $j(3h - 2g)$

4 Expand and simplify these expressions.
- **a** $2x + 3(x + 5)$
- **b** $4d + 2(5d + 6)$
- **c** $9i - 4(i + 2)$
- **d** $7u - 3(2u - 3)$
- **e** $6k + 2e + 3(2k + e)$
- **f** $4a + 7b - 2(5a - 2b)$

Practice

13B Solving equations

1 Solve these equations. Write a mapping for each equation. Then solve the mapping.
- **a** $3t = 18$
- **b** $4u = 32$
- **c** $9p = 27$
- **d** $2h = 13$
- **e** $y + 4 = 16$
- **f** $m - 6 = 11$
- **g** $x + 12 = 30$
- **h** $m - 13 = 28$

2 Solve these equations. Write a mapping for each equation. Then solve the mapping.
- **a** $2x + 5 = 11$
- **b** $4y - 1 = 7$
- **c** $3i + 7 = 25$
- **d** $5n - 25 = 30$
- **e** $9u + 3 = 30$
- **f** $7k - 4 = 31$

3 Mary made some mistakes in her homework. Explain the mistakes and correct them.

- **a** $c + 5 = 12$
  $c \to +5 \to 12$
  $17 \leftarrow +5 \leftarrow 12$
  $c = 17$

- **b** $4b - 8 = 16$
  $b \to -8 \to \times 4 \to 16$
  $12 \leftarrow +8 \leftarrow \div 4 \leftarrow 16$
  $b = 12$

4 Expand the brackets first. Then solve the equation.
- **a** $4(d + 3) = 32$
- **b** $4(t - 2) = 12$
- **c** $5(2s + 1) = 35$
- **d** $3(2g + 10) = 60$
- **e** $3(2f - 1) = 9$
- **f** $3(4q + 5) = 51$

55

13C Constructing equations to solve problems

1 a A book and writing pad cost £8 altogether. The book costs £x.
Write an expression for the cost of the writing pad.

b Maria is twice the age of Janine. Janine is j years old.
Write an expression for the age of Maria.

c The difference between the heights of two trees is 4 m. The taller tree is T metres high. Write an expression for the height of the shorter tree.

2 Solve these problems by creating an equation for each one and then solving it.

a Tyres cost £x each. 4 tyres cost £112.
Find the cost of one tyre.

b Jamie is y years old and Paul is 9 years old. Their ages total 16 years.
How old is Jamie?

c The difference between two numbers is 5.
The larger number is n and the smaller number is 12.
What is the larger number?

d A plum weighs p grams. A lemon weighs 12 g more than the plum.
  i How much does the lemon weigh?
  ii Write an expression for the total weight of the lemon and plum.
  iii If the total weight is 44 g, find the weight of the plum.

e A soap opera lasts 3 times as long as a cartoon.
The cartoon lasts m minutes.
  i How long does the soap opera last?
  ii Write an expression for the total length of the two programmes.
  iii The soap opera and the cartoon last 32 minutes altogether.
  How long does the cartoon last?

f The sum of two consecutive numbers is 51. The smaller number is n.
Find n.

g The sloping side of this parallelogram is 3 cm longer than its base.

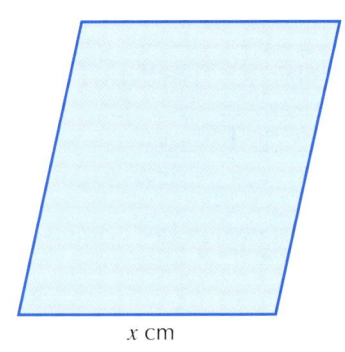

x cm

  i Write an expression for the length of the sloping side.
  ii Write an expression for the perimeter of the parallelogram.
  iii The perimeter of the parallelogram is 42 cm.
  Find the value of x.

Practice

13D Problems with graphs

1 Write down the coordinates of the points on each dotted line.
Then write down the equation of the dotted line.

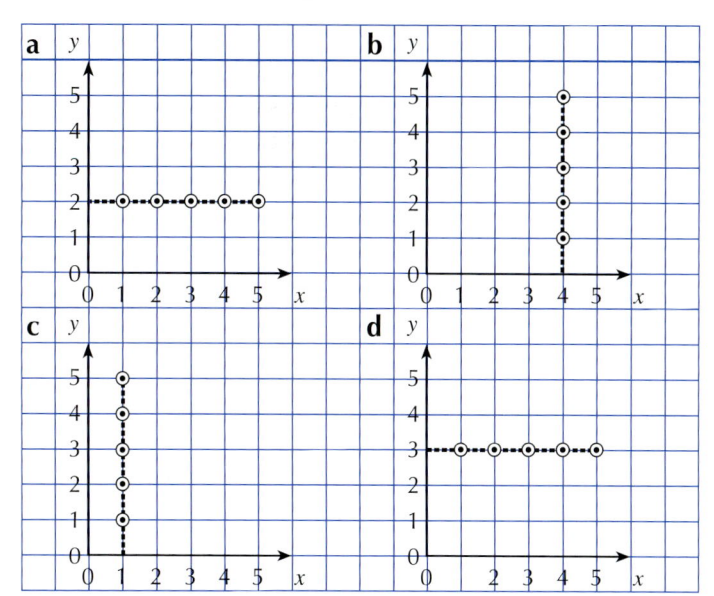

a , **b** , **c** , **d** (grids shown)

2 Use a grid to draw a graph for each of these equations.
Number the axes of your grids from 0 to 6.

 a $x = 4$ **b** $y = 6$ **c** $x = 2$ **d** $y = 1$

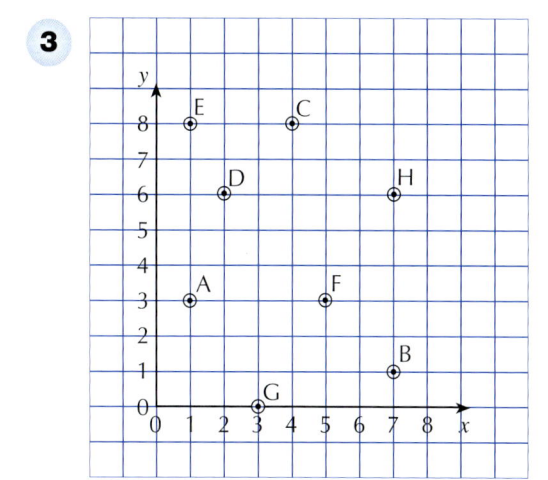

3

Write down the points that lie on each of these lines.

 a $y = 6$ **b** $x = 7$ **c** $y = 1$ **d** $x = 3$ **e** $y = 3$ **f** $x = 1$

4 **a** Draw a grid with each axis numbered from 0 to 6.
 b **i** Mark four points on the x-axis and write down their coordinates.
  ii Write down the equation of the x-axis.
 c **i** Mark four points on the y-axis and write down their coordinates.
  ii Write down the equation of the y-axis.

5 **i** Write down the coordinates of the marked points on each dotted line.

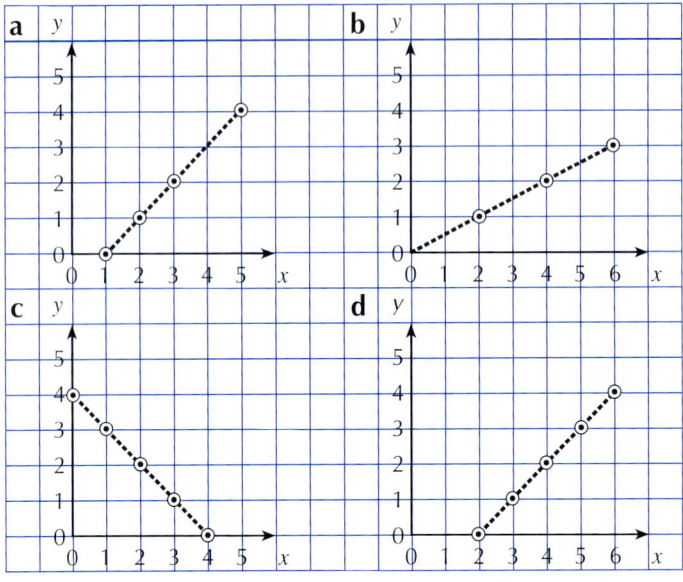

a

b

c

d

ii What is the rule connecting the *x*- and *y*-coordinates?
iii Use algebra to write your rule.

Practice
13E Real-life graphs

1 Sketch a graph to illustrate each of these situations. Label your axes.
  a The height of a person from birth to age 30 years
  b The temperature in summer from midnight to midnight
  c The height of water in a WC cistern from before it is flushed to afterwards

2 This diagram shows the cost of car hire for two companies.

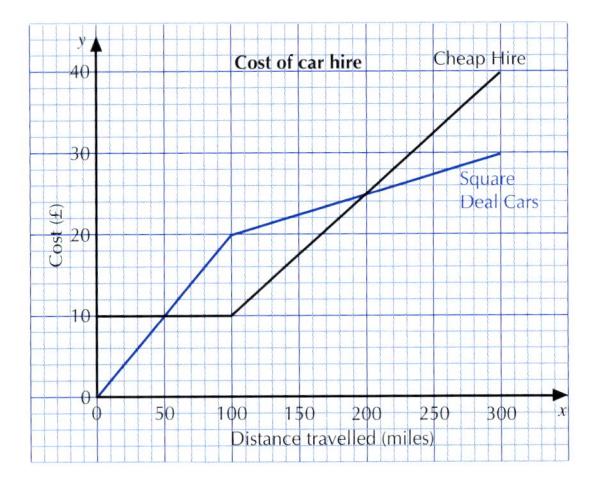

  a Estimate the cost of hiring a car from each company and travelling
    i 60 miles
    ii 100 miles
    iii 240 miles
  b When is Cheap Hire cheaper than Square Deal Cars?

3 Match each description to its graph.

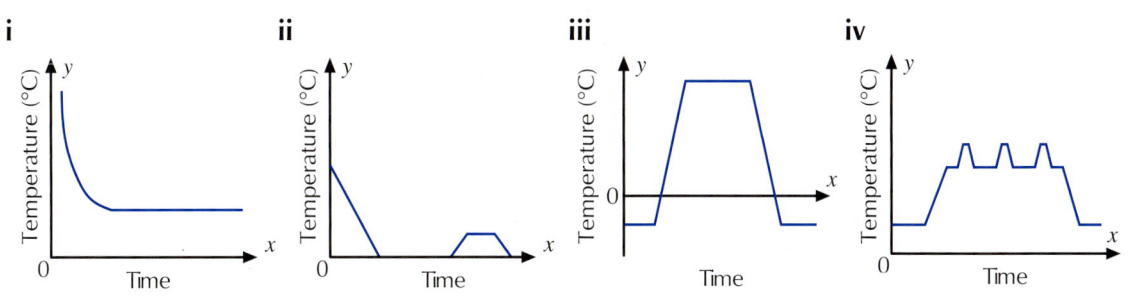

i ii iii iv

a The temperature of the desert over a 24-hour period
b The temperature of a kitchen over a 24-hour period
c The temperature of pond during a month of winter
d The temperature of a cup of tea as it cools down

4 George tried several diets to lose weight. This table shows his weight loss over a one-year period.

Diet	Weight loss/gain
Hay diet	Lost 10 kg in 2 months
Calorie counter	Stayed same weight for 3 months
Vegetarian	Gained 3 kg in 2 months
Usual diet	Gained 12 kg in 1 month
Atkins diet	Lost 28 kg in 4 months

George weighed 105 kg at the beginning of the year.

Draw a graph showing how George's weight changed over time.
Use the horizontal axis for time, with 1 cm to 1 month, from 0 to 12 months.
Use the vertical axis for weight, with 1 cm to 2 kg, from 80 kg to 112 kg.

13F Change of subject

1 Rewrite each of these formulae as indicated.
   a $T = D + H$; express H in terms of T and D.
   b $m = \frac{d}{e}$; express d in terms of m and e.
   c $PV = T$; express P in terms of T and V.
   d $R = r - s$: express r in terms of R and s.

2 Rewrite each of these formulae as indicated.
   a $y = mx$; make m the subject of the formula.
   b $T = 4h - 2$; make h the subject of the formula.
   c $A = C + 2B$; make B the subject of the formula.

3 The perimeter of a shape is given by the formula $P = 4a + 5$.
   a Find the value of P when $a = 4$ cm.
   b Make a the subject of the formula.
   c Calculate the value of a when $P = 41$ cm.

4 A car accelerates for t seconds to a speed of v mph. Its final speed is given by the formula $v = 20 + 4t$.
  a Calculate the final speed of the car if it accelerates for 5 seconds.
  b Make t the subject of the formula.
  c How long does it take for the car to reach a final speed of 80 mph?

5 The formula $A = \dfrac{a+b}{2}$ calculates the average A of two numbers a and b.
  a Find A when $a = 5$ and $b = 9$.
  b Make a the subject of the formula.
  c The average, A, of two numbers, a and 18, is 12.
    Use your formula to find a when $A = 12$ and $b = 18$.

CHAPTER 14 Solving Problems

Practice

14A Number and measures

1 A pen and pencil have a total length of 33 cm. Two pens and a pencil have a total length of 46 cm. What is the length of a pen?

2 Complete these magic squares so that each row and column adds up to 12.

3		7
	6	

1		3
	6	

3 A bag of potatoes in the UK weighs 15 lb.
A bag of potatoes in France weighs 7 kg.
Which is heavier? Use the fact that 1 kg ≈ 2.2 lb.

4 Find two consecutive numbers that add up to 77.

5 Harry's car can travel 320 miles on a full tank of petrol.
He drives 480 km in France. Does he need to stop for petrol?
Use the fact that 5 miles ≈ 8 km.

6 Two 12-hour electric clocks start at 12 noon.
Clock A loses 5 minutes every hour. Clock B keeps perfect time.
  a What will be the time showing on clock A when clock B next reaches 12 o'clock?
  b How long will it take before both clocks show 12 o'clock again?

Practice
14B Using algebra and diagrams to solve problems

1 I am 18 years old.

  a How old was I x years ago?
  b Calculate my age 11 years ago.

2 There are about 30 grams in one ounce.

  a Write a formula, in words, that changes a number of ounces into grams:
  Number of grams =
  b Copy and complete the formula to convert n ounces into G grams:
  $G =$
  c Use your formula to convert 14 ounces to grams.

3 I think of a number, treble it and then subtract 24. The answer is 27.

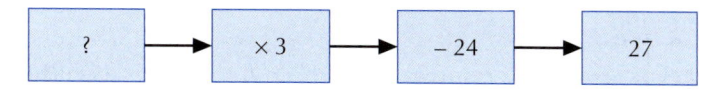

| ? | → | × 3 | → | − 24 | → | 27 |

Work backwards to find the number I first thought of.

4 I think of a number, divide it by 2 and then add 8. The answer is 20.

  a Copy and complete this flow diagram.

| ? | → | | → | | → | 20 |

  b Work backwards to find the number I first thought of.

5 a Fold an A4 sheet of paper in half.
  Open the sheet and count the rectangles.
  b Fold it in half again and count the rectangles.
  c Copy and complete this table.

Number of times paper is folded	Number of rectangles
1	
2	
3	
4	

  d If the paper were folded 5 times, how many rectangles would there be?
  Write down how you could calculate this *without* folding the paper.

14C Logic and proof

Practice

1 Copy and complete these number problems.

a)
```
  2☐
  ☐3
 ---
  5 9
```

b)
```
   7☐
 + 2☐5
 -----
  ☐9 9
```

c)
```
  1 9☐
 - ☐ 2
 -----
  1 3 2
```

d)
```
   4☐
 × ☐9
 -----
  3 8 7
```

2 Give an example to show that the product of three odd numbers is odd.

3 Give an example to show that the product of two odd and two even numbers is even.

4 a Write down the factors of 21.
b Give another example to show that the factors of an odd number are odd.

5 It takes 8 people 12 hours to dig a hole. How long would it take to dig the same hole if there were

a 4 people?   b 2 people?   c 16 people?

6 6 glasses hold 120 cl altogether. 8 mugs hold 144 cl altogether. Which holds the most, a mug or a glass?

14D Proportion

Practice

1 Two of the carriages on a train are first-class. The other six carriages are second-class. What proportion of carriages are first-class?

2 A value pack contains 4 chocolate bars and 8 toffee bars. What proportion of the bars are toffee?

3 One out of every 10 people are left-handed. What proportion are right-handed?

4 Air consists of 4 parts nitrogen to 1 part oxygen. A cupboard contains 50 litres of air.

a How much nitrogen does it contain?
b How much oxygen does it contain?

5 9 light bulbs cost £18. How much does a box of 18 cost?

6 2 gallons is approximately 9 litres.

a How many litres are equivalent to 10 gallons?
b How many gallons are equivalent to 63 litres?

7 8 grams of silver are used to make 12 cm of chain.
  a How much silver does 36 cm of chain contain?
  b How long is a chain that contains 64 grams of silver?

Practice
14E Ratio

1 Simplify these ratios.
  a 12 : 9
  b 16 : 30
  c 18 kg : 42 kg
  d £4 : 75p
  e 8 weeks : 12 days
  f 45 cm : 3 m
  g 5 kg : 1.75 kg

2 a Divide 40 cm in the ratio 7 : 1.
  b Divide 600 mm in the ratio 11 : 9.
  c Divide 5000 people in the ratio 3 : 5.
  d Divide £76 in the ratio 2 : 7 : 10.

3 Donna eats three times more hot meals than cold meals. She eats 96 meals in July. How many of them were hot?

4 The ratio of children Year 8 who own a mobile phone to those that don't is 3 : 2. There are 210 children in Year 8.
How many children do *not* own a mobile phone?

5 The land area to sea area of the surface of the Earth is in the ratio 3 : 7. The total surface area of the Earth is 500 000 000 km^2.
What is the area of land?

CHAPTER 15 Shape, Space and Measures 4

Practice
15A Plans and elevations

1 Draw each of these 3D shapes on an isometric grid.

a 2 cm, 3 cm, 5 cm

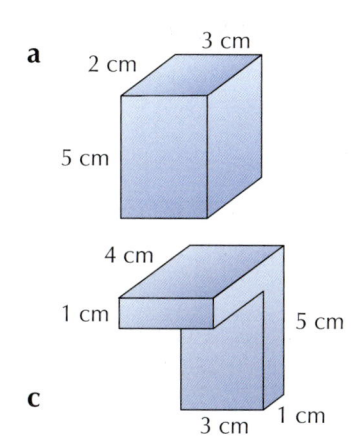

b 8 cm, 5 cm, 2 cm

c 4 cm, 1 cm, 5 cm, 3 cm, 1 cm

d 2 cm, 1 cm, 1 cm, 1 cm, 1 cm, 3 cm, 3 cm

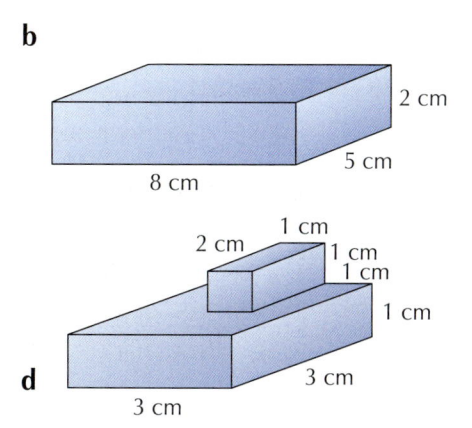

2 For each of these 3D shapes, draw a
  i plan   ii front elevation   iii side elevation

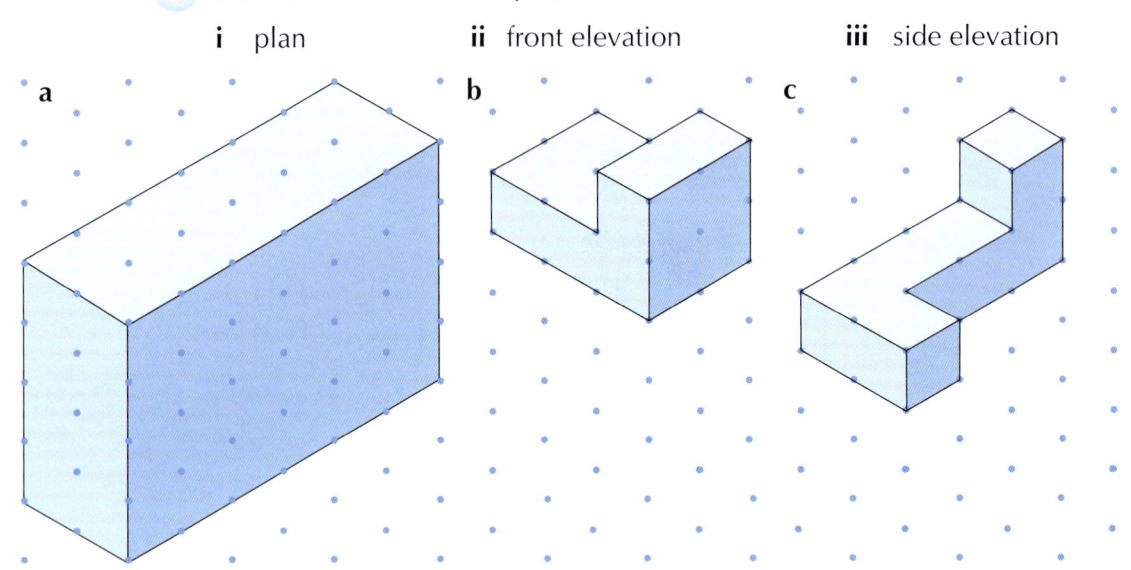

a   b   c

3 The plan, front and side elevations of a 3D shape are shown below. Draw the solid on an isometric grid.

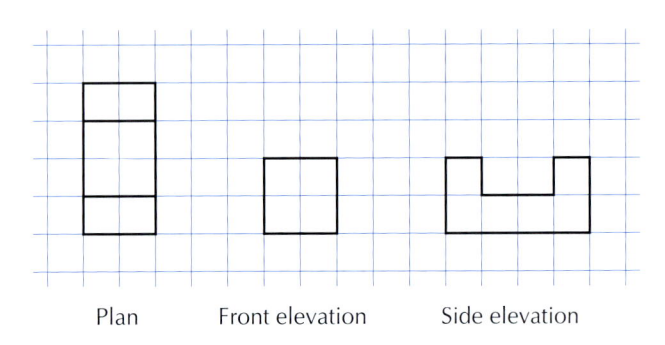

Plan   Front elevation   Side elevation

Practice

15B Scale drawings

1 These objects have been drawn using the scales shown. Find the true lengths of the objects.

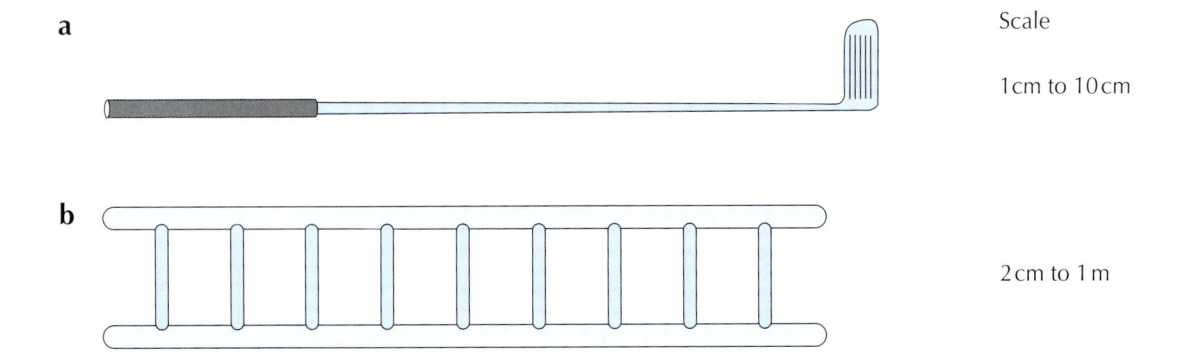

a

Scale

1 cm to 10 cm

b

2 cm to 1 m

64

c

1 cm to 0.7 m

d

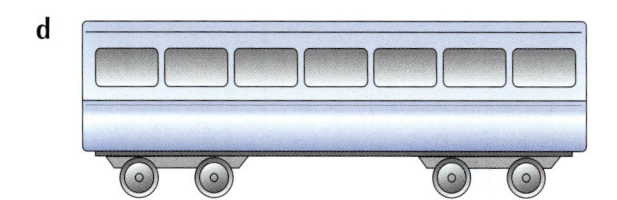

2 cm to 3 m

2 This diagram shows a scale drawing of an aircraft hanger.

Scale: 1 cm to 120 m

   a Calculate the real length of the hanger.
   b Calculate the real width of the hanger.
   c Calculate the area of the hanger.

3 Copy and complete this table.

	Scale	Scaled length	Actual length
a	1 cm to 2 m		24 m
b	1 cm to 5 km	9.2 cm	
c		6 cm	42 miles
d	5 cm to 8 m	30 cm	

4 This diagram shows a scale drawing of a supermarket.

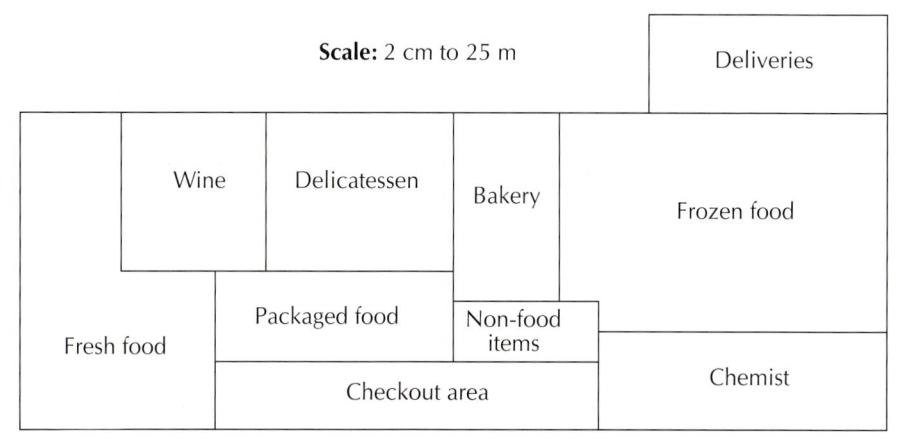

Scale: 2 cm to 25 m

Make a table showing the dimensions and area of each section of the supermarket.

15 Practice

15C Coordinates in all four quadrants

1 Write down the coordinates of the points A, B, C, D and E.

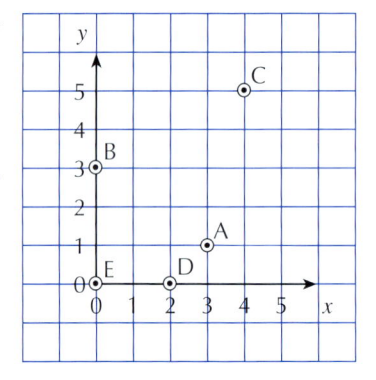

2 a Make a copy of the grid in Question 1 and plot new points A(1, 1), B(3, 1) and C(5, 4).
  b The three points, A, B and C, are the vertices of a parallelogram. Plot the point D to complete the parallelogram.

3 Write down the coordinates of the points G, H, I, J, K, L and M.

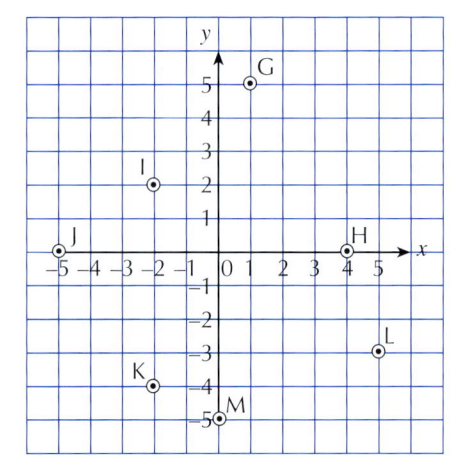

4 a Make a copy of the grid in Question 3 and plot new points G(–5, –3), H(–5, 4), I(2, 4)
  b Join the points, G, H and I, to make a triangle.
  c Plot point J so that GHIJ is a square. Draw the other two sides of the square.
  d The diagonal, GI, of the square crosses the axes at two points. Write down their coordinates.

Practice

15D Constructing triangles

1 Construct these triangles. Label your daigrams.

a 7 cm, 6 cm, 9 cm

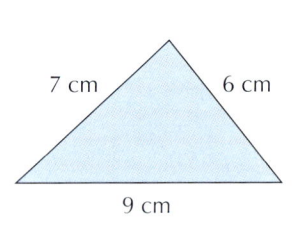

b 9.5 cm, 7 cm, 3.5 cm

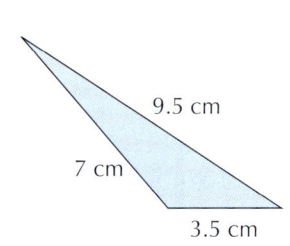

c 8.8 cm, 6.5 cm, 8.8 cm

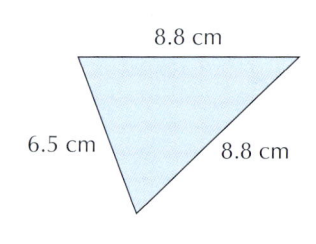

2 Construct each of these triangles. Describe the type of triangle you have drawn: acute-angled, right-angled, obtuse-angled, scalene, isosceles, equilateral.
  Hint: Make a rough sketch of the triangle before you draw it accurately.
  a △ABC where AB = 9 cm, BC = 7 cm and AC = 7 cm
  b △PQR where PQ = 7.2 cm, QR = 3.4 cm and PR = 9.1 cm

3 Construct these triangles using ruler, compasses and a protractor.

a — 70°, 70°, 5 cm

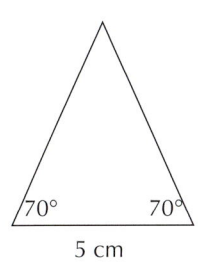

b — right angle, 35°, 6.5 cm

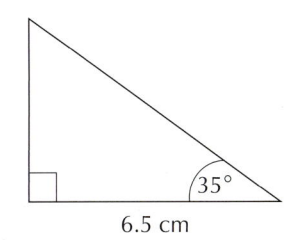

c — 117°, 38°, 3.8 cm

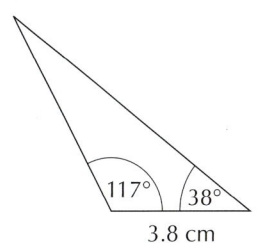

Practice

15E Loci

1 Sketch loci for these. Describe each locus.

  a A moving garden swing

  b A moving ski lift chair

2 This diagram shows three wooden balls in a game of bowls. Trace the diagram.

  a A fourth ball, D, moves equidistant from balls A and B. Sketch its locus.

  b A fifth ball collides with the balls. Ball C moves so that it is equidistant from the edge of the bowling green. Sketch the locus.

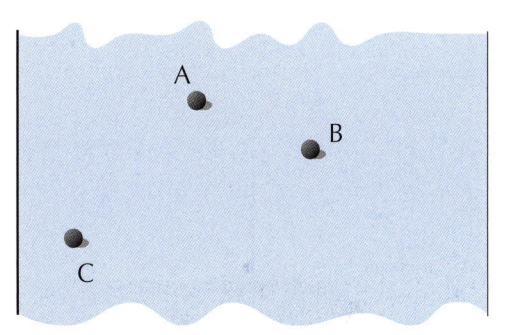

3 This diagram shows two motorways and some towns. Trace the diagram.

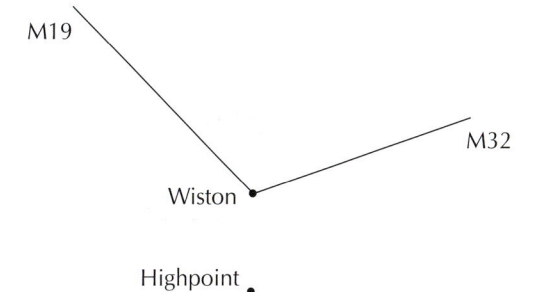

M19, M32, Wiston, Highpoint

Stan drives his car from Highpoint, keeping the same distance from Wiston. When Stan is equidistant from the two motorways, he drives away from Wiston, keeping equidistant from the motorways.
Sketch the locus of Stan's car.

15

4 Mark a point on the circumference of a 2p coin. Move the coin along the edge of a ruler. Draw the locus of the marked point.

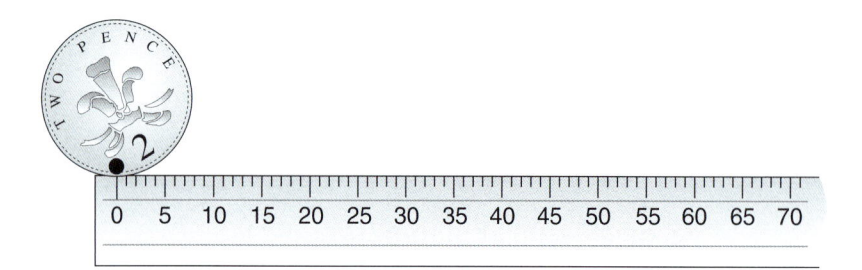

Practice

15F Bearings

1 Use your protractor to find the marked angles. Write down the bearing of B from A. **Remember:** Use three figures.

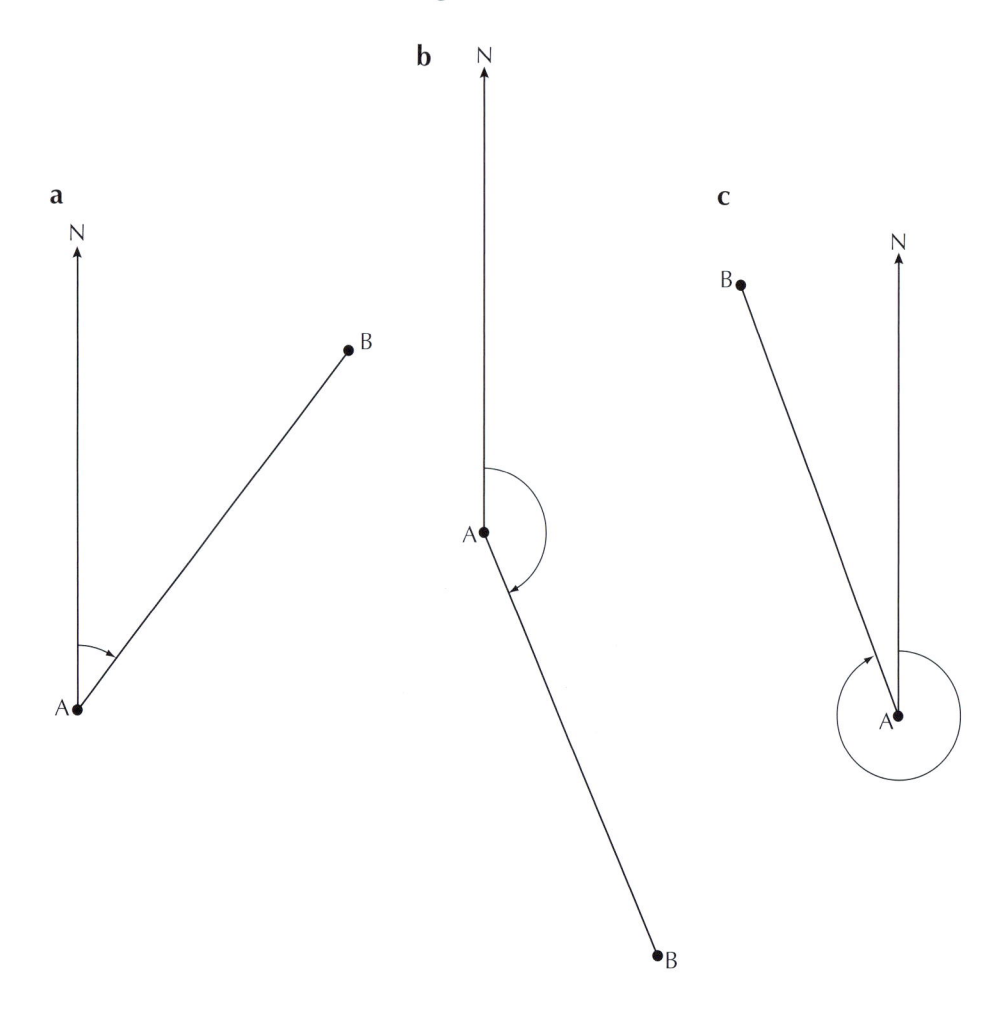

a

b

c

68

2 Find the bearing of P from Q.

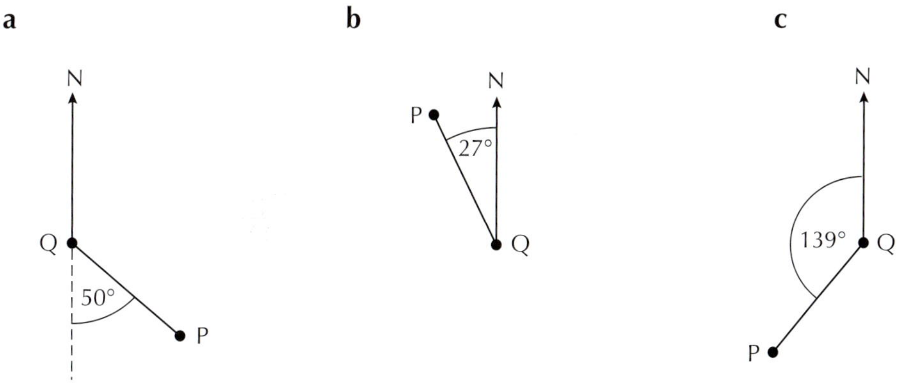

   a   **b**   **c**

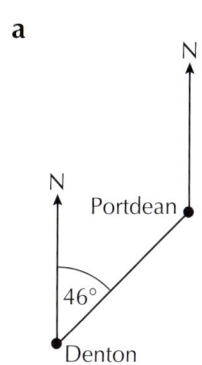

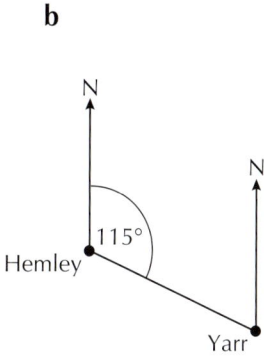

3

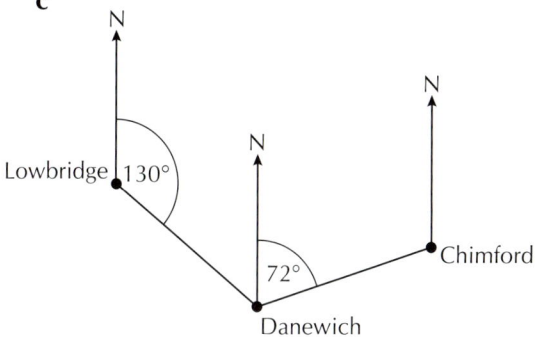

Calculate the bearing of

   a Portdean from Denton   **b** Denton from Portdean
   c Yarr from Hemley   **d** Hemley from Yarr
   e Chimford from Danewich   **f** Danewich from Chimford
   g Danewich from Lowbridge   **h** Lowbridge from Danewich

4 Sketch these bearings. Label your diagrams.

   a A skier is on a bearing of 72° from the ski lodge.
   b Clerkhill is 12 miles from Moffat on a bearing of 115°.

CHAPTER 16 Handling Data 3

Practice

16A Frequency tables

1 This table shows the lengths of some python snakes, measured to the nearest metre.

Length of snake (m)	Frequency
0 – 1	2
2 – 4	4
5 – 8	7
9 – 11	9

a One of the snakes is 6 m long. Which class contains this length?
b How many snakes are shorter than 5 metres?
c How many snakes have a length of 5 metres or more?
d How many snakes are between 2 and 8 metres long, inclusive?
e How many snakes were measured?

Five more snakes are measured.
Their lengths are 3 m, 8 m, 4 m, 1 m and 10 m.

f Copy and update the table to include these five snakes.

2 These are the durations of 30 telephone calls.

4	12	8	1	19	7	7	28	14	54
9	2	20	16	2	43	5	18	1	5
5	14	9	10	3	30	11	6	17	2

Times have been rounded up to the nearest minute.
Copy and complete this table.

Length of telephone call (minutes)	Tally	Frequency
1 – 10		
11 – 20		
21 – 30		
31 – 40		
41 – 50		
51 – 60		

3 These are the volumes of liquid contained in 20 coconuts, measured in millilitres.

| 12.0 | 11.1 | 10.5 | 12.8 | 12.0 | 10.1 | 11.8 | 12.3 | 10.7 | 12.7 |
| 10.0 | 11.6 | 12.1 | 10.5 | 10.8 | 12.6 | 10.7 | 11.4 | 12.8 | 11.3 |

Copy and complete this frequency table.

Volume of liquid (ml)	Number of coconuts
10.0 – 10.4	
10.5 – 10.9	
11.0 – 11.4	
11.5 – 11.9	
12.0 – 12.4	
12.5 – 12.9	

Practice

16B The median

1 Find the median of these sets of data.
Remember: Order the numbers from smallest to largest.

a 9, 3, 4, 8, 9, 4, 4
b 30, 20, 20, 70, 45, 10, 55, 30, 60, 25, 90
c £28, £83, £19, £44, £20, £71, £43, £16, £99
d 5 m, 7.5 m, 1 m, 3.5 m, 6.5 m

2 Find the median of these sets of data.

a 5, 5, 0, 2, 2, 4
b 23, 21, 19, 21, 21, 21, 18, 25
c 8 kg, 4 kg, 9 kg, 9 kg, 6 kg, 12 kg, 4 kg, 3 kg, 9 kg, 9 kg
d 300 mm, 100 mm, 250 mm, 600 mm, 400 mm, 800 mm

3 a Write down a set of three numbers whose median is 4.
b Write down a set of four numbers whose median is 4.
c Write down a set of seven numbers whose median is 20.

4 This table shows the points scored by eight robots in school Robot Wars.

Robot	Score
Buzz Chainsaw	78
Cracker	23
Flipper	55
Electro	37
Fireball 2	83
Ram Rod	46
Speedy	71
Pounder	50

a Calculate the median score.
b If Ram Rod had scored 50 points, would the median change?

5 Sara found that the median number of children in 10 families was 3.5. How many families had 3 or fewer children?

16 Practice
16C Constructing frequency diagrams

1 This table shows which method of transport pupils enjoyed the most.

Method of transport	Number of pupils
Roller skates	5
Bicycle	12
Skateboard	9
Scooter	7

Construct a bar chart for the data.

2 This table shows the numbers of goals scored in some football matches.

Number of goals	Number of matches
0	8
1	13
2	20
3	18
4	15
5	7

Construct a bar-line graph for the data.

3 This table shows the times some runners took to complete a 10-km race.

Time taken (minutes)	Number of runners
20 – 39	6
40 – 59	13
60 – 79	24
80 – 99	38
100 – 119	20

Construct a bar chart.

Practice
16D Comparing averages and ranges

1 QuickDrive and Ground Works are two companies that lay drives. The numbers of days they take to complete 9 similar drives are shown below.

QuickDrive	2, 5, 3, 3, 6, 2, 1, 8, 3
Ground Works	3, 2, 3, 1, 4, 3, 2, 2, 1

a i Calculate the mode for each company.
   ii Compare the modes.
b i Calculate the median for each company.
   ii Compare the medians.
c i Calculate the range for each company.
   ii Compare the ranges.
d Which company is the most consistent?

2 This table shows the weights of fish three anglers caught in a competition.

Jerry	Aditya	Marion
230 g	230 g	100 g
100 g	400 g	130 g
380 g	280 g	430 g
720 g	320 g	200 g
450 g	250 g	70 g
		180 g
		200 g
		90 g

a i Calculate the range for each of the anglers.
   ii Who was the most consistent? Explain your answer.
b i Calculate the median for each of the anglers.
   ii Who performed the best overall? Explain your answer.
c Which angler would you choose to enter a competition that offered prizes for the heaviest fish caught? Explain your answer.

3 This table shows the mean and range of the weekly rainfall in two holiday resorts.

	Larmidor	Tutu Island
Mean	6.5 mm	5 mm
Range	33 mm	62 mm

Explain the advantages of each island's climate using the mean and range.

16E When to use different averages

1 The average of each set of data has been given.
Do you think the average is suitable? Explain your answer.

   a 5, 5, 7, 9, 9, 9, 10, 12   mode = 9
   b 3, 4, 4, 5, 5, 7, 100, 200   mean = 41
   c 1, 1, 2, 2, 3, 8, 100   median = 2
   d 21, 22, 24, 24, 25   mean = 23
   e 7, 7, 8, 9, 10   mode = 7
   f 0, 1, 1, 2, 20, 20, 21   median = 2

2 For each set of data, decide whether the range is suitable or not. Explain your answer.

   a 4, 6, 6, 8, 10, 12
   b 3, 6, 7, 8, 9, 50
   c 1, 80, 80, 82, 84

3 Judges awarded these points to competitors in a surfing competition.

   12, 14, 14, 24, 28, 33, 36, 39, 40, 42, 48

   a i   Calculate the mean. Is this a suitable measure of average?
      ii Calculate the median. Is this a suitable measure of average?
      iii Calculate the mode. Is this a suitable measure of average?
   b Calculate the range. Is this measure suitable? Explain your answer.

4 Two shops offer these sizes of dresses.

Periwinkle	12, 14, 16, 18, 30
Jenny's	10, 12, 14, 16, 18, 20, 22

   a Which shop has the greatest range of sizes?
   b Do you think the range is a suitable measure? Explain your answer.

16F Experimental and theoretical probability

1 There are four possible results of flipping two ordinary coins at the same time.

a   What is the theoretical probability of flipping two heads? Write your answer as a decimal.
b   Flip two coins 20 times and record the results.
c   Calculate the experimental probability of flipping two heads. Write your answer as a decimal.
d   Compare the experimental and theoretical probabilities. Are they close?
e   How could you obtain a closer experimental probability?

2 Lena arranged these raffle tickets in three rows for people to choose from.

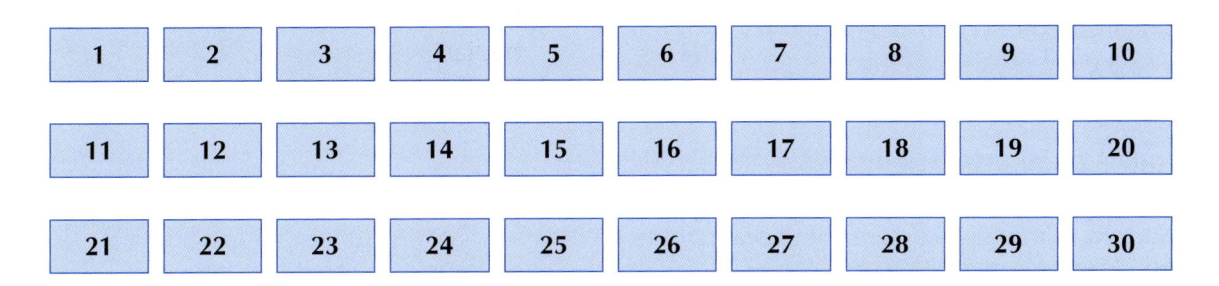

1	2	3	4	5	6	7	8	9	10
11	12	13	14	15	16	17	18	19	20
21	22	23	24	25	26	27	28	29	30

She predicted that people are more likely to choose a number from the middle row than the outer rows.

a   What is the theoretical probability of someone choosing a number from the middle row?
b   Design and carry out an investigation to test Lena's prediction.

Published by HarperCollins*Publishers* Limited
77–85 Fulham Palace Road
Hammersmith
London
W6 8JB

> www.**Collins**Education.com
> Online support for schools and colleges

© HarperCollins*Publishers* Ltd 2003

10 9 8 7 6 5 4 3

ISBN 0 00 713871 7

Andrew Edmondson asserts the moral right to be identified as the author of this work. All rights reserved. No part of this publication may be reproduced, stored in a retrieval system, or transmitted in any form or by any means, electronic, mechanical, photocopying, recording or otherwise, without either the prior permission of the Publisher or a licence permitting restricted copying in the United Kingdom issued by the Copyright Licensing Agency Ltd., 90 Tottenham Court Road, London W1P 9HE.

British Library Cataloguing in Publication Data
A Catalogue record for this publication is available from the British Library

Edited by First Class Publishing
Project Management by Sam Holmes
Covers by Tim Byrne
Designed and illustrated by Barking Dog Art
Production by Emma Johnson
Printed and bound by Printing Express Ltd, Hong Kong

The publishers would like to thank the many teachers and advisers whose feedback helped to shape *Maths Frameworking*.

Every effort has been made to trace copyright holders and to obtain their permission for the use of copyright material. The author and publishers will gladly receive any information enabling them to rectify any error or omission in subsequent editions.

> You might also like to visit:
> www.harpercollins.co.uk
> The book lover's website